IT HAPPENED IN

GEORGIA

IT HAPPENED IN

GEORGIA

Stories of Events and People that
**SHAPED PEACH STATE
HISTORY**

Third Edition

JAMES A.
CRUTCHFIELD

Globe
Pequot GUILFORD, CONNECTICUT

Globe
Pequot

An imprint of The Rowman & Littlefield Publishing Group, Inc.
4501 Forbes Blvd., Ste. 200
Lanham, MD 20706
www.rowman.com

Distributed by NATIONAL BOOK NETWORK

Copyright © 2020 The Rowman & Littlefield Publishing Group, Inc.

Map by The Rowman & Littlefield Publishing Group, Inc.

British Library Cataloguing in Publication Information available

Library of Congress Cataloging-in-Publication Data available

ISBN 978-1-4930-3947-0 (paperback)
ISBN 978-1-4930-3948-7 (e-book)

∞™ The paper used in this publication meets the minimum requirements of American National Standard for Information Sciences—Permanence of Paper for Printed Library Materials, ANSI/NISO Z39.48-1992.

To the memories of Alice S. Hawthorne and Melih
Uzunyol, who died in the bombing at the Summer
Olympic Games in Atlanta, July 1996

CONTENTS

PREFACE

This book highlights several fascinating episodes of Georgia history. It begins with the life and times of Ocmulgee, a prehistoric Indian town, and ends with the tragic bombing at the 1996 Summer Olympic Games in Atlanta. Each story is complete in and of itself and may be read individually or out of sequence.

Although these vignettes don't in any way purport to be a thorough history of the state, they have been selected to give the reader a broad understanding of the historical background of "The Empire State of the South."

I hope that *It Happened in Georgia* will provide you with a few hours of pleasure and that it will, perhaps, find its way into the classrooms of the state, thereby giving younger generations a better appreciation of their vast heritage.

CIRCA AD 1500

The Last Days
of Ocmulgee

The sun's shadows were lengthening as warm days became cool evenings. By the European calendar it was late September, but to the hundreds of American Indians gathered in their ceremonial plaza, it was time for the Busk. This ritual, sometimes known as the Green Corn ceremony, derived its name from the Muskogean word, *baskita*, which means "to fast." The Busk celebrated the ripening of the Indians' most important crop—corn—and was a time for purification and renewal.

In the early Georgia town of Ocmulgee, which was located near present-day Macon, the Busk lasted for about a week, and the inhabitants fasted almost until the end of the celebration. Throughout the week, they participated in songs, dances, and games to celebrate the new crop and the new year. Then, as the Busk drew to a close, all the fires in the village were extinguished so they could be relit from the sacred flame.

A fire maker who had been specially appointed for the celebration arranged several logs and built the new sacred fire. When the fire maker signaled that the new flame was ready for distribution, his assistants lit torches from the master fire, then went around to every house and temple in Ocmulgee and rekindled the fires of the village. Then, the feasting began in earnest, and before the evening was over, every man, woman, and child in the village had filled his or her stomach with fresh, sweet corn.

As part of the purification process, chief priests visited families and forgave their sins. All debts were forgiven and any grievances were resolved. Everyone performed rituals of purification such as cleaning out lodges, bathing, or taking cathartic medicines. Families laid plans for the future and a new year was thus begun.

Today, two of America's most impressive prehistoric sites lie within Georgia's boundaries. Ocmulgee National Monument was the first large prehistoric ruin in the South to be scientifically excavated. Almost as imposing is the Etowah Indian Mounds State Historic Site, located near Cartersville, north of Atlanta. The Etowah remains have been designated as a national landmark, and the complex consists of several mounds dominated by three unusually large ones. The large mounds probably provided the base for the dwellings of the chief priests and other high-ranking officials of the village.

Both the Ocmulgee and Etowah sites are examples of an early American Indian culture known as Mississippian, which reached its zenith in early Georgia from about AD 700 to AD 1500. The Mississippian period is characterized by the numerous large temple mounds and huge agricultural villages that sprang up throughout the valley of the Mississippi River and its tributaries. When the fires of Mississippian brilliance were extinguished, shortly before the explorations of the Spanish conquistador Hernando de Soto, the lands of the South fell into a dark age that lasted until the rise of new tribes: the Cherokees, Creeks, Chickasaws, and Choctaws.

Georgia is the twenty-first-largest state in land area in the United States, and the largest state east of the Mississippi River. It covers 57,906 square miles, which is just over 37 million acres. Its extreme east-west breadth is 250 miles, and its extreme north-south length is 315 miles.

Mississippian settlements in early Georgia were located in the floodplains of rivers. These floodplains offered rich soil for growing corn, squash, and beans. The vegetables provided the Indians with a surplus of food, which, in turn, allowed them to give up their hunter-gatherer societies and establish permanent settlements. In these settlements, they established trading systems with neighboring villages, made elaborate handicrafts, and held religious ceremonies.

Most Mississippian towns were built around a central ceremonial plaza, which was the center of government and religious life. Villagers would gather in the plaza for ceremonies such as the Busk. Surrounding the plaza were large, flat-topped mounds where temples or homes were built for the chief priests. The common people lived in earth lodges, and their social standing was reflected by how close their dwelling was to the ceremonial plaza. It was during Mississippian times that southeastern Indian culture reached a high level of accomplishment.

By the mid-1500s the Mississippian way of life had vanished forever. No Europeans ever witnessed the eerie beauty of a sacred Mississippian-era Busk ceremony or visited a chief priest atop a high temple mound. All that is left today of this once powerful culture—a culture that in its own way rivaled those of the Incas and the Aztecs—are mysterious remains, some of which can be seen at the Ocmulgee and Etowah historic sites in Georgia.

1737

The Wesley Brothers' Brief Stay in Georgia

The late days of autumn, 1737, were trying ones for John Wesley. The thirty-four-year-old preacher was looking for a way to get out of Savannah in one piece. When just two weeks earlier, entangled in immense legal difficulties, he publicly announced that he would leave Georgia forever, he was threatened with immediate arrest if he dared depart the colony. But, warnings aside, Wesley wrote:

> I now saw clearly the hour was [*sic*] come for me to fly for my life, leaving this place, and as soon as evening prayers were over, about eight o'clock, the tide then serving, I shook off the dust of my feet, and left Georgia, having preached the Gospel there with much weakness indeed and many infirmities, not as I ought but as I was able.

On December 2, tired of his tenure in Georgia, Wesley boarded a craft destined for Charleston. Several days later he was bound for England, while law enforcement officials in Savannah scratched their heads over his sudden disappearance.

Wesley's sojourn in Savannah had been a brief one, less than two years. He and his younger brother, Charles, likewise a preacher, had arrived in the colony in February 1736, in the company of Georgia's founder and chief benefactor, Governor James Oglethorpe. Oglethorpe had known the Wesley family for years back in England. His desire to establish Protestant missions among the Indians and to provide a source of spiritual guidance for his own colonists prompted him to offer the Wesley brothers a berth on the ship, *Simmonds*, before he departed England on his second trip to Georgia.

Oglethorpe's generous offer intrigued both John and Charles Wesley. John's entire life had centered around religion, and he had been ordained a priest in the Church of England nine years earlier. Although not a youngster any longer, he was more than anxious to travel to foreign shores and try his powers of conversion on the Indians. But John had another motive for making the transatlantic journey. Before his departure from England, he wrote to a friend, confessing that "My chief motive is the hope of saving my own soul. I hope to learn the true sense of the Gospel of Christ by preaching it to the heathen."

Brother Charles possessed deep religious convictions as well, although his faith was not as intense as John's, nor did he have the desire to spend several years in Georgia. In later years, after his return to England from his journey in America, Charles confessed that:

I took my degree, and only thought of spending all my days in Oxford. But my brother, who always had the ascendant over me, persuaded me to accompany him and Mr. Oglethorpe to Georgia. I exceedingly dreaded entering into Holy Orders but he overruled me here also, and I was ordained deacon by the Bishop of Oxford, and the next Sunday, priest by the Bishop of London.

Both Wesley brothers decided to accompany Governor Oglethorpe to Georgia. John was to be paid an annual salary of fifty pounds to serve as "Minister to Savannah and Missionary to the Indians," and Charles to function as private secretary to Oglethorpe. The governor's party left England on December 10, 1735, and for the next two months, the Wesleys used the ship's passengers—much to the chagrin of the captive audience—as a testing ground for their ministrations in Georgia in the months that lay ahead.

During the voyage, the brothers became entangled with two women who eventually would cause them much dismay. The ladies were on their way with their husbands to a new life in Georgia. Beatre Hawkins, wife of Dr. Thomas Hawkins, and Anne Welch, wife of John Welch, decided that in order to entertain themselves during the long voyage across the Atlantic, they would delude John Wesley into believing that he was saving their souls.

Georgia has 100 miles of Atlantic Ocean shoreline.

7

For days and weeks on end, Wesley labored with the women through sermon after sermon about sin and the need for redemption. Charles Wesley and several of John's friends saw through the charade and warned John that the women were merely toying with him. However, serious-minded John would not listen to the criticism and continued his preaching. By the time the ship had reached Savannah harbor, the

two women had turned hostile to Wesley, most likely because the innocent preacher had failed to respond to their amorous advances.

A week after arriving in Savannah, Charles was sent to a new town called Frederica, located several miles to the south on St. Simons Island. Hawkins and Welch, already relocated there with their husbands, immediately launched a devious plot, accusing Wesley of adultery. Charles quickly fell out of grace with the governor and eventually pleaded with John to come to his rescue. In the meantime, however, John stayed in Savannah and began his church duties in earnest. He soon became known as a zealot and, according to one churchgoer, he "drenched his parishioners with the physic of an intolerant discipline," and his sermons "tended to propagate a Spirit of Indolence and of Hypocrisy."

John finally made the trip to Frederica to check on his brother. In time he convinced Oglethorpe that the vicious women had lied, and he generally smoothed out the difficulties between Charles and the governor. Still, Oglethorpe deemed it best that Charles leave Georgia for good and return to England, which he did in August 1736. With his mission accomplished, John returned to Savannah to take over the pulpit at Christ Church.

While preaching at Christ Church, John became infatuated with an eighteen-year-old girl named Sophia Hopkins. Although he actually considered asking for her hand in marriage, all of Wesley's closest friends advised against it. Wrestling with his emotions, the preacher distanced himself from Sophia for a while, hoping that the proper course of action would be divinely revealed to him. While the two were apart, however, Sophia married another, and John became increasingly hostile toward her, even to the point of refusing to serve her communion.

Wesley was quickly served with a warrant for refusing Sophia the sacraments. He was also sued by Sophia's husband for one thousand pounds. Two weeks later John was hauled into court before a grand jury that had been rigged by Sophia's uncle. Accused of a number of offenses, Wesley was indicted on all counts. As he awaited his trial, he decided to flee Savannah and Georgia once and for all.

After making his harrowing escape, and while sailing back to England, Wesley reflected on what he considered to be his massive failure in Georgia.

> I went to America to convert the Indians; but oh! who shall convert me! This have I learned in the ends of the earth, that I am fallen short of the glory of God, that my whole heart is altogether corrupt and abominable, and consequently my whole life. Alienated as I am from the life of God, I am a child of wrath, an heir of hell.

Time soon healed Wesley's emotional and spiritual wounds. Less than two years after his return to England, he organized the Methodist Church, a denomination that had spread all the way to the backwoods of America before his death in 1791 at the age of eighty-six. Brother Charles remained active during that period as well. Before he died in 1788, he had written more than 6,500 church hymns, many of them still performed in today's Methodist churches across the world.

1742

The Battle of Bloody Marsh

Don Manuel de Montiano watched proudly as column after column of brightly uniformed soldiers disembarked from the fleet of thirty-six ships that lay offshore the southwestern tip of St. Simons Island. Montiano—the Spanish governor of Florida—and his flotilla had departed St. Augustine just a few days earlier with orders from the governor-general of Cuba to drive the English not only from St. Simons itself but from the entire ten-year-old colony of Georgia. After taking over Savannah, the Spanish forces intended to attack Charleston in hopes that they would succeed in expelling the English from South Carolina as well.

Montiano spent most of July 5, 1742, supervising the unloading of men and equipment on St. Simons Island. A few of the ships in the Spanish fleet required some minor repair work as a result of cannon fire from a nearby English fort as the ships sailed through the narrow channel to the point of debarkation. The governor happily noted that little damage had been done, however, and his spirits soared even more when he received intelligence that the English had deserted the fort and retreated northward to nearby Fort Frederica and its surrounding village, also called Frederica. By July 7, Montiano assessed that all was ready, and he issued orders to prepare for the march across the island to attack the English.

The mean elevation of Georgia is 600 feet. The highest point in the state is Brasstown Bald, which has an altitude of 4,784 feet.

Since Montiano was unfamiliar with the terrain of the island and not at all certain how many troops occupied Fort Frederica, he decided initially to send out only two small patrols to reconnoiter the countryside and to spy out the fort. Accordingly, during the early morning hours of July 7, he ordered Captain Nicholas Hernandez, accompanied by twenty-five soldiers and forty Yamassee Indians who were allies of the Spanish, and Captain Sebastian Sanchez, commanding fifty men, to proceed northward toward Fort Frederica. By mid-morning the two advancing groups had hacked their way through the swampy and insect-infested undergrowth that covered the island and joined forces at a spot less than 2 miles from the fort. There, they literally ran into five Georgia militiamen who were out on patrol duty themselves.

In a brief skirmish, William Small, one of the Georgia militiamen, was killed outright by Spanish gunfire, while his four companions managed to escape and make their way back to Fort Frederica. The excited soldiers met with forty-three-year-old James Oglethorpe, the founder and governor of Georgia as well as the commander of the fort. Oglethorpe quickly organized a mixed command of his own soldiers, supplemented by Creek and Yamacraw Indians, and hastily headed south down the narrow pathway leading out of Fort Frederica. Less than an hour later, Oglethorpe's forces and the two Spanish patrols met head to head at a spot about a mile from Fort Frederica. The sudden appearance of the small English army startled the Spanish soldiers and fighting ensued. Within minutes, thirty-six men from the Spanish contingents were either killed or missing in action, and the two commanders themselves, Captains Hernandez and Sanchez, were captured. The remaining members of Governor Montiano's scouting parties retreated toward the main Spanish encampment on the southern end of the island. When Oglethorpe called for a casualty report of his own men, he learned that only one of his soldiers had been killed during the fighting due to heat exhaustion.

It was around noon when the Spanish survivors straggled into Montiano's camp and reported to the shocked governor. Greatly dismayed over the outcome of this first encounter with the English in their own territory, Montiano sent for Captain Antonio Barba, a seasoned veteran of many battles in Cuba, and ordered him to organize a force consisting of three companies of his own Havana-based regiment. The column of two hundred men was quickly dispatched northward to rescue any patrol members who might have been cut off from retreat.

While Montiano was reorganizing his forces, Oglethorpe was not idle. After the mid-morning skirmish with the

Spanish patrols, the English governor marched his army down the trail to a large swampy area located 5 miles south of Fort Frederica. There, on the northern side of the marsh and beneath huge old oak trees covered with spidery Spanish moss, Oglethorpe ordered his men to gather downed tree trunks and brush and pile them together to form barricades from which the riflemen could shoot while remaining hidden.

It was a hurried project and had to be completed before the angered Spanish army started back up the trail on an invasion course. When the task was finally completed, Oglethorpe studied the terrain once again, content that the only route the advancing Spanish could take would be along the narrow causeway that crossed the marsh and passed directly in front of the camouflaged barricades. Oglethorpe placed Captain Raymond Demere along with sixty men on one side of the emerging trail and stationed Captain Charles Mackay's contingent of forty men on the other. He then headed back to Fort Frederica to recruit more men and arms, hoping to return before the Spanish arrived.

The English did not have to wait long. Around three in the afternoon, amid a light rain that did nothing but accentuate the intense humidity already present, the English soldiers, without Oglethorpe, heard their Spanish adversaries crossing the marsh. English muskets and rifles boomed, and Spanish troops fell left and right. By the time Captain Barba realized that his small army had been ambushed, he had already lost several soldiers to the gunfire. He ordered a hasty retreat back across the marsh, but the fighting continued for about another hour.

Oglethorpe was on his way back to the marsh with reinforcements when he was met by part of his command that had prematurely retreated during the turmoil and confusion.

Soon after he reached the rest of his army at the swamp, the Spanish retreated back to their home base at the other end of the island.

The brief confrontation between English and Spanish armies on that hot July day at Bloody Marsh, as the encounter was later called, ended Spain's dreams of reclaiming the infant English colony of Georgia. It was the most important battle in the War of Jenkins's Ear—the hostilities that had existed between the two countries since 1739. Governor Montiano and his soldiers soon left St. Simons Island and returned to St. Augustine. James Oglethorpe was recalled to his native England the following year to be tried by court-martial for his handling of military affairs in Georgia. He was acquitted of all charges. The former governor never returned to Georgia but later served in Parliament and eventually retired from the army as a general. According to one of his biographers, he was "a man of fine feeling, of excellent taste, and of culture far beyond the men of his class." The "Father of Georgia" died in England in 1785.

1755

Acadians in Georgia

In late December 1755, a few hundred Georgians gathered on the wharf at Savannah and watched intently as two British frigates sailed up the Savannah River. When the ships came within range, their captains signaled the landing and requested permission to dock. For days stories had been circulating all over Savannah about the imminent arrival of the ships. What interested the town's residents most was the boats' cargoes, rumored to be French-speaking Acadians from the one-time French, but now British, colony of Nova Scotia.

Approval to come ashore was given, and the curious spectators watched as nearly four hundred French men, women, and children disembarked from the ships. There were a mixture of emotions among the Georgians, since, technically, these new arrivals were their enemies, due to the fact that England had been at war with France for a year and a half. But at the same time, it saddened some to observe the Acadians, who were unable to utter a word in English, were obviously very poor, and were exchanging frightened looks with each other as they milled about in the crowd.

Although far removed from the hostilities that raged between the French and English in the conflict commonly called the French and Indian War, the Savannah townspeople were still cognizant of the seriousness of the affair. Most correctly perceived that whichever side emerged victorious would claim practically all of North America to the ultimate exclusion of the other. And, so far, affairs had not been going too well for the English. Six months earlier, the supreme British commander in America, General Edward Braddock, had been killed in the Ohio country while attempting to wrest Fort Duquesne from the French. But to offset that defeat, they had just recently received the good news that British redcoats had defeated the French at the Battle of Lake George in New York in September.

Suspicious of so many people of French extraction in his colony and concerned that they might contribute to the cause of their military kinsmen in a time of war, Nova Scotia's English governor, Charles Lawrence unilaterally made the decision to expel all French nationals from his colony. Numbering close to ten thousand people, the innocent Acadian farmers and their families were loaded into British ships, sent southward along the Atlantic coast, and dumped in any American colony that would accept them. Massachusetts, Maryland, Connecticut, New York, Pennsylvania, North and South Carolina, and Georgia all accepted the vagabonds.

Georgia's colonial governor, John Reynolds, was the man who would make all of the decisions relative to the disposition of the unwanted Acadians in Georgia. He was in Augusta negotiating with Creek and Cherokee Indians, but he decided that his presence in Savannah was more important. Immediately returning to the coast to address the problem at hand, he quickly decided to allow the Acadians to stay in the vicinity for ten days. To assist in their well-being, the governor ordered that each individual be issued a pound of rice. In the meantime Reynolds conferred with his council of advisors, and a decision was made to disperse the four hundred foreigners to several communities along the seaboard so that it would be impossible for large numbers of them to congregate and plan mischief for the residents of Savannah.

Ten days passed, and some success had been achieved in the dispersal plan. But apparently little had been done to ensure that they leave town in due time. At the end of the second week after their arrival, the council received appeals from a number of the Acadians, declaring that they were experiencing "a Sick and Languishing Condition," and that they were "incapable of Supporting themselves and families." They added that they would surely "perish" if additional assistance was not provided.

The governor and council responded by issuing more food, but at the same time, they were trying to figure out a way to get the emigrants to leave. The Catholic religion of the Acadians was the issue that most bothered government officials as well as the populace at large. "They were all Papists & consequently enemies to our Religion & Government & unfit to be suffered to remain in such a very weak & defenceless Colony as Georgia," Reynolds wrote.

When Henry Ellis replaced Reynolds as governor a year later, the Acadians were still present in the Savannah area, attempting to scratch out a living from the soil. Finally, in February 1757, the Georgia Assembly passed an act that addressed the Acadian problem and offered what it hoped would be solutions that satisfied Georgians and French alike.

The act was called "For the providing for & disposing of the Acadians now in this Province," and it allowed for the distribution of the Acadians to various parts of the colony where they could work on plantations for their subsistence. If they refused to follow these direc- tives, they were subject to the laws of indentured servitude. By late spring it appeared that the displaced French would adjust to conditions in Georgia, and Governor Ellis proudly noted that they were proving to be "very useful to the Colony" and even advocated assimilating the Acadian population into mainstream Georgian society. Within the year, however, bad times hit again and the emigrants were forced to ask for additional government assistance. Ellis personally guaranteed that he would give seeds to the newcomers if the council would issue them free land.

For whatever reasons—whether Governor Ellis's land distribution program was never implemented or because the Acadians simply failed to blend in with the primarily English-speaking population of Georgia—the Acadians did not prosper. Gradually, family by family, they left the colony. Some journeyed to South Carolina and others went to Mobile and New Orleans on the Gulf Coast. By 1763, the same year that the Treaty of Paris ended the North American conflict between Great Britain and France, only thirty-seven Acadian families remained in Georgia.

According to an August 1763 issue of the Savannah newspaper, the *Georgia Gazette*, "a number of Acadians who have been here for a few years" left their homes bound for the island of Santo Domingo. In December the same journal reported, "All the Acadians here are about leaving the place; yesterday upwards of 90 of them went on board a vessel in the river to Cape Francois [Santo Domingo]." The last Acadian families departed from Savannah in mid-January 1764, thus ending the difficult and trying sojourn for these innocent people in Georgia.

1777

Dueling Statesmen

Button Gwinnett, a forty-two-year-old plantation owner, former governor of Georgia, and one of only three signers of the Declaration of Independence from Georgia, spoke in low tones with a distinctively English accent that clearly belied his birthplace. A strikingly handsome man, with dark eyes and long hair that draped around his shoulders, Gwinnett was well-schooled and had conscientiously used his education to represent his adopted state in the Continental Congress.

Another gentleman, General Lachlan McIntosh—displaying considerable more flamboyance than Gwinnett—originally hailed from Scotland. Ten years Gwinnett's senior, McIntosh, the quintessential military man, had lived in Georgia since he was eleven years old when his father came from

England with General James Oglethorpe to establish the colony. Neatly dressed in his striking army uniform, the general sported graying hair that was tied up in the back in a queue, or in today's vernacular, a ponytail.

Gwinnett and McIntosh had come together that day in 1777 to fight a duel. The men had never been on particularly good terms, and serious political differences between them had only served to strain relations further. Always in turmoil, the pot finally boiled over on May 15, 1777—before all the members of the State Assembly—when General McIntosh called Button Gwinnett "a scoundrel and a lying rascal." After conferring with friends and political associates, Gwinnett decided that the only way he could restore his honor was to challenge McIntosh to a duel. Accordingly, an invitation was extended to the general, who accepted. No time was wasted. The duel was set for early the following morning.

George Wells and Major Joseph Habersham, the two seconds whom Gwinnett and McIntosh had selected, decided that the duel should be fought with pistols and made the necessary arrangements for a brace of finely designed flintlocks to be furnished by McIntosh.

Before daybreak on May 16, Gwinnett and Wells strolled up to the site of the anticipated duel, a meadow located less than a mile from Savannah on the property of the last colonial governor of Georgia. There, they found that McIntosh and Habersham had already arrived. The four men exchanged polite greetings but participated in no additional conversation other than the upcoming duel. McIntosh and Habersham opened a beautifully decorated wooden box, extracted the two pistols that were housed inside, and passed them to Gwinnett and Wells to inspect. Nodding their approval, they handed the weapons back to Habersham, who, in the presence of Wells, carefully loaded the pistols with powder and a single ball each.

Rumors of the upcoming duel had rapidly circulated throughout Savannah, and even at this early hour, several people had arrived to witness the event. Uncomfortable with the growing audience, the two parties decided to move the site of the duel a few yards across the meadow, beyond a stand of trees, to a place not viewable by the crowd.

The time had come to discuss the distance that would be paced off before a shot could be fired. Wells and Habersham asked the duelists' pleasure. Gwinnett answered first, stating that he would accept "Whatever distance the General pleases." McIntosh opined that "eight or ten feet would be sufficient." The final distance was measured at four paces, or approximately 12 feet. When the seconds suggested that Gwinnett and McIntosh simply face away from each other at the selected distance, then, upon command, turn and fire, the general exclaimed, "By no means. Let us see what we are about."

The geographical center of Georgia is located about 17.5 miles southeast of Macon.

Gwinnett and McIntosh took up their positions facing each other at a distance of four paces. One of the seconds roared, "Fire," and the two men pulled the trigger of their weapons almost simultaneously. The prominent "plop" sound of lead tearing into flesh resounded across the meadow. Gwinnett fell, grabbing one of his legs, and exclaimed, "My thigh is broken!" McIntosh, also hit in the leg, disregarded his own wound and called out to Gwinnett, asking him if he was up to reloading and repeating the exercise. Gwinnett replied that he was most certainly willing to have another go at it if he could be assisted in standing up. Wells and Habersham quickly stepped between the men and refused to allow a second shot. Declaring that both men's honor had been upheld, they assisted the wounded duelists to their carriages and sent them home for medical care.

Probably prompted by the extremely hot weather for the time of the year, infection, followed by gangrene, rapidly attacked Gwinnett's wounded leg, and within three days, he was dead. McIntosh recovered slowly and lived another three decades, going on to serve with distinction in the Revolutionary War.

News of Button Gwinnett's death spread rapidly throughout the South. On May 26, an article describing the dueling incident appeared in the *South Carolina Gazette*.

An unhappy dispute having lately arisen between the Hon. Button Gwinnett, Esq., late Governor of Georgia, and General M'Intosh, the commanding officer of the Continental Troops in that State, the same was determined by a Duel between the Parties, with Pistols ... when both the Combatants were wounded. Mr. Gwinnett died of his wound ... and the General, we hear, lay dangerously ill.

Lyman Hall, one of the other two signers of the Declaration of Independence from Georgia, was devastated by the

death of his friend, Button Gwinnett. In a letter written a
month after the duel, he wrote to a friend:

> O Liberty! Why do you suffer so many of your faith-
> ful sons, your warmest votaries, to fall at your shrine!
> Alas my friend! My friend!! ... Excuse me, Dear Sir,
> the Man was Valuable, so attached to the Liberty of
> this State and Continent that his whole attention,
> influence and interest circled in it and seemed riv-
> eted to it. He left a mournful widow and daughter &
> I may say the Friends of Liberty on a whole Conti-
> nent to deplore his Fall.

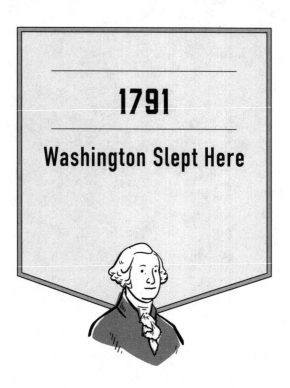

1791

Washington Slept Here

Wednesday, May 18, 1791, was an exciting day for the eleven hundred residents of Augusta, Georgia. The small village perched along the banks of the Savannah River had been made the state capital just six years earlier but now boasted nearly three hundred dwellings, an academy capable of accommodating ninety students, the statehouse, a church, a courthouse, a jail, and several tobacco warehouses. What caused all the excitement this day was the fact that Augusta, situated in the back country 110 miles upstream from Savannah, had been deemed important enough to be visited by President George Washington.

As President Washington's entourage pulled up to the outskirts of Augusta, he was met by Governor Edward Telfair and other dignitaries. It would be a reunion for Washington and Telfair since their friendship dated from the days the governor had served in the Continental Congress.

The trappings of the presidential party were a sight to behold. Washington's personal, spotless, white coach was pulled by four stately horses and accompanied by a baggage wagon led by two horses, four additional saddle horses, and a military contingent that had been sent out days earlier to meet the president in Savannah and to escort him to Augusta. The soldiers were members of the local volunteer militia, and according to one observer, "They cut a very superb appearance . . . their uniforms being blue, faced with red and laced with silver, their caps and other accoutrements equal to their uniforms and the horses nearly of a color and in good order."

This was Washington's second major journey away from the national seat of government since he had become the country's first president two years earlier. The first trip, completed in 1789, was a visit to the northeastern section of the United States. Following his return to his offices, Washington had overseen the relocation of the capital from New York City to Philadelphia and had also begun discussions and planning to move it again from Philadelphia to a newly developed plot of land along the Potomac River called the District of Columbia. In March 1791, at the end of his first two years in office and following the adjournment of the first session of Congress, the fifty-nine-year-old president decided to visit several southern states.

Georgia has the eighth-largest population in the United States, with a 2018 figure of 10,429,379.

Although Washington's trips to the Northeast and the South turned out to be partially social in nature, his primary reason for visiting the two regions was to demonstrate a sense of national unity. After the Revolutionary War, in which he had played such a significant role, Washington had retired to his plantation near Alexandria, Virginia. However, rapid growing pains and increasing dissatisfaction with the way the newly formed United States government was operating under the Articles of Confederation caused a great deal of consternation among delegates from the various thirteen states. In an attempt to stabilize the nation, Washington had come out of retirement to preside over the Constitutional Convention held in 1787. After that gathering, which set the tone for future governmental affairs, he had been selected to be the first president.

President Washington left Philadelphia on March 21, 1791, writing to his friend, the Marquis de Lafayette, "I shall enter on the practice of your friendly prescription of exercise, intending ... to begin a journey to the southward, during which I propose visiting all the Southern States." From Philadelphia, Washington traveled along the rudimentary road system that stretched down the Atlantic Coast close to the shore, stopping and visiting hamlets and villages along the way, until he reached Savannah. Enjoying a few days there, he left town on May 14 to visit the governor and the people of Augusta.

The day after he left Savannah, Washington visited Mulberry Grove, the plantation of Mrs. Nathanael Greene, widow of the noted Revolutionary War general. General Greene had been one of Washington's most trusted lieutenants during the Revolutionary War, and after the conflict, he had established Mulberry Grove along the Savannah River just a few miles out of town on land given to him by a grateful Georgia government. When he died unexpectedly in 1786, he left his wife and five small children with a sizable debt, and Mrs. Greene had struggled to keep the plantation intact. Although President Washington was most concerned about the widow's welfare, he left a simple journal entry describing his visit: "Called upon Mrs. Greene . . . and asked her how she did."

Two days after leaving Mulberry Grove, the president stopped overnight at Waynesborough, "a small place, but the Seat of the Court of Burkes County." He described the village as containing only about eight houses but went on to write that attempts were under way to organize an academy. On the following day, May 18, Washington's party began what turned out to be a busy day for all concerned when it was met by the governor and other officials and leading citizens from Augusta.

After exchanging pleasantries with the governor, the president mounted one of the horses that had accompanied his carriage, and "was escorted into the Town & recd. under a discharge of Artillery." By now, it was afternoon, and if Washington entertained ideas of getting any rest after the ride into town, he was sorely mistaken. He was advised that the governor was hosting a "large and brilliant dinner" at four o'clock at his own plantation, The Grove. Before dinner all present lifted their glasses as fifteen separate toasts were given for everything from the sacredness of the Fourth of July, to Burgoyne's defeat at Saratoga, to Washington's victory over the British at Yorktown, to the memory of the late General Greene. Completing the long day was a ball, hosted by Mrs. Telfair, "to the Ladies," to which the exhausted president attended "for a short time."

Early on the following morning, a group of interested citizens wrote a message to President Washington in which they:

> ... present[ed] their congratulations upon your arrival here in health, with the assurance that it will be their greatest pleasure, during your stay with them, to testify the sincere affection they have for your person, their sense of obligation for your merits and for your services, and their entire confidence in you as the Chief Magistrate of their country.

Washington responded to the townspeople in a letter he wrote later in the day in which he thanked them "for your congratulations on my arrival in Augusta with great pleasure."

During the afternoon of May 19, Washington viewed the Augusta Volunteer Light Horse Regiment, a parade, an artillery salute, and then attended "an elegant dinner," highlighted by fifteen more toasts, among them one calling for "Improvements and extension to the navigation and commerce of Georgia." May 20 was busy for the president as he toured plantations in the Augusta area, observed the falls of the Savannah River, and attended a private dinner party hosted by Governor Telfair.

At six o'clock on the morning of May 21, President Washington left Augusta. Thanking all of those citizens who were involved in making his stay a pleasant one, the president and his entourage crossed the Savannah River amid a final artillery salute. Affairs in Augusta gradually returned to normal, with its residents elated to have been visited by a hero of the Revolutionary War and their country's first president.

JAMES VANN

[C. 1768–1809]

James Vann was one of the wealthiest and most influential leaders of the Cherokee people during the late 1700s and early 1800s. Born in Georgia a short distance from Diamond Hill, his future plantation near present-day Chatsworth, his ancestry included both Scots and Cherokee heritage, which allowed the boy to grow up in more-affluent circumstances than other Cherokee children. As a young man, Vann battled fiercely with westward-moving white frontiersmen encroaching on ancient Cherokee land, and soon came to realize that the Cherokees and the whites could never coexist. He was a man of many moods, described by journalist John Howard Payne—who spent considerable time among the Cherokees—as "aristocratic, impetuous, and full of chivalric daring." A more recent historian, Henry Thompson Malone, called him "a peculiar combination of benevolent leader and rip-snorting hoodlum."

However he appeared to his neighbors and scholars across the ages, he realized early on that the benefits to be derived from a missionary presence among the Cherokees was absolutely imperative for his tribe's future, and especially for the young people, if the Cherokees were ever to integrate with the white man's world. In 1801, at Vann's invitation, Moravian missionaries from Salem, North Carolina, established Springplace Mission on property near the site of his future home, a structure that was replaced by his son, Joseph, several years later with the brick residence that is today the centerpiece of the Chief Vann House State Historic Site. Vann was an astute businessman, building his plantation into a several-hundred-acre showplace that was reputedly the largest in the Cherokee Nation. He was a large slaveholder and at one time owned hundreds of cattle and horses. He persuaded the government to run a federal highway across his property and later benefited immensely from the decision, as traffic increased along the route. After an inebriated Vann was violently murdered in 1809 in a roadside tavern by person (or persons) unknown, his estate was divided between his wife, Margaret, and his favorite son, Joseph.

1792

The Invention of
the Cotton Gin

If anyone was ever down on his luck, it was surely twenty-six-year-old Eli Whitney. Sitting on the verandah of Mrs. Nathanael Greene's beautiful plantation house, Mulberry Grove, located just outside Savannah, Whitney contemplated the chain of events that had brought him, a Massachusetts "Yankee," to the Deep South. He had graduated from Yale College only a few months earlier and had been lured to Georgia in anticipation of filling a tutoring position that promised to pay well enough to get him out of the large debt he had incurred while putting himself through school. But alas, when he arrived in Savannah, he learned that his employer intended to pay him only half of the previously agreed upon salary. The kindhearted Mrs. Greene, widow of the famed Revolutionary War general, insisted that he stay on her plantation until he could find more work.

It was a hot summer's day in 1792 as Whitney and Phineas Miller, Greene's caretaker, discussed ideas that might make them some money. Miller was also interested in a project that would help Greene recover from the heavy debt that she found herself in trying to operate her large, but only marginally profitable, plantation. The subject soon turned to cotton.

Cotton was in large demand in England for use in the manufacture of fine cloth. However, the variety that was grown in Georgia and neighboring states—and the type that could be easily processed by machine—only grew in the lowlands near the ocean, and production of marketable quantities was very limited. Whitney was told that another kind of cotton, "short-staple," was easy to grow anywhere in the warm, moist climes of the South. The only problem with the short-staple variety was the extreme difficulty in separating the seeds from the fiber. The machine used with the other variety didn't work on short-staple cotton, and consequently, it required one person's labor for a full day to produce one pound of marketable, seed-free cotton. If only someone could come up with a device to automatically remove the seeds from the fiber, the growing of cotton could bring an economic boon to farmers all over the region.

That day on Greene's sprawling front porch was a turning point in Eli Whitney's life. The young teacher was excited about the conversations he had pursued with Phineas Miller and other discussions like them with various plantation owners and overseers in the region. During the next few weeks, the notion that there must be some easy, inexpensive way to extract the cotton seeds from the fiber preyed on his mind.

Finally, after hours of daydreaming and trial-and-error design work, he produced a prototype cotton gin that performed the desired functions without a hitch. Explaining the chain of events that had occurred since he arrived in Georgia to his father, the contented inventor wrote:

> There were a number of very respectable gentlemen ... who all agreed that if a machine could be invented which would gin the cotton with expedition, it would be a great thing both to the country and to the inventor. In about ten days I made a little model, for which I was offered, if I would give up all right and title to it, a Hundred Guineas. I concluded to relinquish my school and turn my attention to perfecting the machine. I made one ... with which one man will clean ten times as much cotton as he can in any other way before known.

Whitney and Miller soon became partners and told the nearby Georgia landowners that their goal was to build enough cotton gins to place them at convenient places throughout the region, thus allowing a grower to bring in his cotton, have it processed, and pay for it with a share of the "clean" fiber. Now, amid glowing success, a serious problem arose. The demand for the new machines outgrew the ability of the two men to build them. Whitney returned to New England, where he hired skilled labor to manufacture the gins en masse, while Miller stayed in Georgia handling the administrative and logistical aspects of the new partnership.

It soon occurred to Whitney that his cotton gin, as revolutionary as it was, would be extremely easy to reproduce if some unscrupulous person had the notion. Whitney and Miller had been careful not to divulge details of their design to anyone and even refused to allow cotton growers to watch the gin while it processed their cotton. Accordingly, in June 1793, Whitney applied for a patent on his machine. In the application he proudly wrote "That with the Ginn [*sic*], if turned with horses or by water, two persons will clean enough cotton in one day, as a hundred persons could clean in the same time with ginns now in common use."

More problems were to beset Miller and Whitney. In March 1795, fire destroyed Whitney's New Haven, Connecticut, factory where the cotton gins were manufactured. A disheartened, but resolute, Whitney ruefully declared:

> For more than two years, I have spared no pains nor exertion to systematize and arrange my business in a proper manner. This object I have just accomplished. It was the purchase of many a toilsome day and sleepless night. But my prospects are all blasted and my labor lost. I do not, however, despair and I hope I shall not sink under my misfortune. I shall reestablish the business as soon as possible but it must be a long time before I can repair my loss.

As events turned out, poor Eli Whitney never "repaired" his loss. Struggling to recover from the severe damages—both emotional and economic—caused by the fire, he watched helplessly as dozens of counterfeit cotton gins flooded the marketplace. His only recourse was to go to court, and before the ordeal was over, he had sixty lawsuits pending against those who had stolen his design. All of his erstwhile efforts, however, were to little avail. Although the state of South Carolina, after years of delay, finally awarded him a settlement of $50,000, authorities in Georgia denied that he was the inventor of the cotton gin in the first place! The final straw came when the US Congress, spearheaded by several of its southern members, refused Whitney the right to renew his patent when the time came.

Eli Whitney finally threw in the towel. The fire that destroyed his New Haven factory, the endless law-suits—most of them ruled against him—and the tre-mendous debt that he and his partner had acquired as they started their business proved to be too much for the men to continue. Eli never returned to Georgia, turning his atten-

tions instead to the plausibility of mass-producing firearms, a business that eventually made him a wealthy man.

Despite Eli Whitney's failure to garner personal success from the invention of the cotton gin, his accomplishment caused such an impact on the South that cotton soon became the entire region's number-one cash crop. Fewer than two hundred thousand pounds of cotton were exported in 1791, when the tedious work of separating the plant's seeds from the fiber was still largely performed by hand. A dozen years later, southern growers were selling forty-one million pounds of cotton a year, and the plant had become the basis for the "plantation" economy that had spread over much of the South in the days before the Civil War.

1795

Indian Trade on the St. Mary's River

It is ironic that the United States of America—known today throughout the world as the bulwark of capitalism and free enterprise—should have proposed and propagated, from its very beginnings, a system of trade with the native population wherein total control was vested with the federal government. During 1795, however, a remote spot in the swamplands of extreme southeastern Georgia was selected to become the first of two sites to implement an ambitious, well-intentioned project in nationalism. It was called the "Factory System," and before its demise almost thirty years later, it oversaw the operation of a number of trading posts located all over the region east of the Mississippi River, as well as a few in the trans-Mississippi West.

Early on in his first administration, President George Washington foresaw the need for an Indian policy that would bring various tribes under the influence of the infant United States government. Fulfilling the day-to-day needs of the natives appeared to be a good way to accomplish the mission. As early as 1793, in a message to Congress, Washington had strongly suggested that "the establishment of commerce with the Indian nations, on behalf of the United States, is most likely to conciliate their attachment," but added that "[the trade] ought to be conducted without fraud, without extortion, with constant and plentiful supplies, with a ready market for the commodities of the Indians, and a stated price for what they give in payment and receive in exchange."

The president's plea fell on deaf ears. During the following year, he renewed his efforts to establish a meaningful trading system with the natives. "I cannot refrain from again pressing upon your deliberations the plan which I recommended at the last session for the improvement of harmony with all the Indians within our limits by the fixing and conducting of trading houses," he declared, this time prompting the formation of a congressional committee to explore his recommendations. On March 3, 1795, after being convinced that most of the tribes would fall under British influence if some kind of trading system was not immediately implemented, Congress finally passed a bill to study the feasibility of Washington's idea. The following year, the establishment of the Factory System became a reality.

During the first decade of its existence, the system operated loosely under the direction of the US secretary of war. In 1806, the "Office of the Superintendent of Indian Trade" was created to report directly to the secretary. Offices were maintained in Philadelphia until 1807, when they moved to Washington, DC.

The system provided for the operation among various Indian tribes of a number of government-run Indian stores, or factories, eventually numbering twenty-eight, mostly in frontier regions with few white settlers. The stores were to be stocked with all types of top-quality trade goods in which the Indians would have an interest, including rifles, powder, balls, hunting knives, hatchets, cooking pots and utensils, sewing supplies and cloth, beads, trinkets, and much more. The natives, in exchange for these goods, would gladly swap their furs and deer hides, both items in high demand back east. Simply stated, the system, according to early historian Reuben Gold Thwaites, "was an attempt to conduct the Indian trade by government agents, and to give the Indians the benefit of fair dealing, and of goods at cost price." It is interesting to note, however, that, although the factory system—and, therefore, the US government—would theoretically be the major player in any future fur trade opportunities that might develop with the Indian nations, private trappers and traders were not prohibited from freelancing in the business as long as they were properly licensed.

> The coldest temperature ever recorded in Georgia was 17 degrees Fahrenheit below zero on January 27, 1940, in Floyd County.

The selected site in Georgia for the first factory was Colerain, located just east of Okefenokee Swamp on the north bank of St. Mary's River, the dividing line between Georgia and Spanish Florida. The post's customers were to be the Creek Indians, a powerful Muskogean-speaking tribe whose several thousand members frequented large areas of present-day central and southern Georgia and Alabama, but whose closest primary villages were located a couple of hundred miles away. For several years, British fur traders stationed out of Pensacola, Florida, had monopolized the Creek trade, and American government officials were particularly anxious to make inroads in this potentially dangerous relationship.

When the newly appointed factor (or chief agent), Edward Price, arrived at his post at Colerain on January 11, 1796, he described it as "a store 60 feet by 28 feet on one story, half of which had no floor in it." He then complained that

> [s]oldiers had been pilfering the government goods. A strong tendency toward liquor existed among all classes. Neither corn nor any other products from the soil were to be had. It was impossible to purchase milk, vegetables, poultry or even fish. The inhabitants of the country presented a wretched appearance. . . .

The factory at Colerain survived only eighteen months as a government fur post, its success greatly hindered by its distance from the Creek villages. Over the years, its operations were moved to several other locations across Georgia—Fort Wilkinson, Ocmulgee, Fort Hawkins, and Fort Mitchell— before permanently closing operations in 1819. Throughout its tenure, the Creek factory and its successors were plagued by underperformance and poor profits. Toward the end of the 1816 trading season, for example, its warehouse contained only $43 worth of furs and peltries. The history of Colerain factory pretty much reflects the experience of most of the other factories that would be opened across the nation in future years.

Before its demise the Factory System operated fur posts, at one time or another, in the present-day states of Georgia, Tennessee, Alabama, Indiana, Michigan, Ohio, Illinois, Wisconsin, Iowa, Missouri, Arkansas, and Louisiana. Fur trade historians have identified a number of reasons the Factory System failed, among them the following, in no particular order or degree of relevance:

1. The prohibition of allowing liquor in the Indian trade, a practice often commonly used among the competitor private fur companies.

2. The prohibition of the extension of credit by fur factors to their Indian customers.

3. Because factories were supplied only with American-made trading goods, the quality of such goods was oftentimes inferior to those imported by the private companies.

4. Employees of private companies, as well as free trappers, were allowed to participate in the fur trade in direct competition with the government, so long as the participants were properly licensed.

5. The adverse impact of the War of 1812, which permanently closed many government factories, but which had little effect on the private companies.

6. The inexperience of the United States government participating in a complex industry such

as the fur trade, in comparison with the business acumen of the private companies' management.

Over the years, the Factory System made many enemies, the most vocal, and damaging, being the American Fur Company, a far-ranging outfit owned by John Jacob Astor. As early as 1813, Astor's chief lieutenant, Ramsay Crooks, expressed his contempt of the government operations when he wrote to his employer that "the Gentlemen who vote appropriations to carry on a traffic of no real benefit to our tawny neighbors ... will discover how fallacious were their expectation," adding that the very Indians best served by the system were "the first to raise the tomahawk against the American settlements."

By 1822, shortly after he took his new seat in the US Senate, Thomas Hart Benton of Missouri doomed the Factory System once and for all. Benton was strongly influenced by Astor spokesman Ramsay Crooks, and soon introduced legislation in Congress to disband the government operation, thus allowing companies, such as American Fur, to privatize—and monopolize—the lucrative fur trade as newer and more-rewarding areas of pristine wilderness were being exploited along the upper Missouri River and in the Rocky Mountains.

By this time, the Factory System was suffering from a combination of mismanagement, poor performance, dwindling fur-bearing animal populations in the East, and lukewarm public support, prompting Congress to gladly support Benton's proposal. It was, therefore, no surprise to most Americans when they learned that, on May 6, 1822, President James Monroe had signed the bill abolishing the Factory System. What may have amazed them, however—had they been familiar with all of the facts at the time—is that the

43

System had operated twenty-eight factories located throughout practically the entire eastern United States and extending more than 100 miles west of the Mississippi River, and that during its period of operation, it had gone a long way toward ameliorating relations between the United States and several of its Indian tribes.

Much to the chagrin of Astor and Crooks, almost two and a half years passed before the last factory closed and all accounting activity for the system reconciled. During the interval, Crooks persistently hounded Senator Benton to be sure that the legislation closing down the Factory System was not being circumvented.

During the Factory System's brief life, hundreds of thousands of dollars' worth of trade goods were exchanged with various Indian tribes in return for rich, luxuriant furs, which in turn were transported to Eastern markets for processing and, in some cases, exportation to Europe. Had the Factory System been ultimately successful, it would have provided a vehicle for much smoother Anglo-Indian relations in the future, and could have provided the fledgling United States with a source of substantial, badly needed, income. The policy's eventual failure not only jeopardized the homogeneity of the two races, but also left the door open to the vast trans–Mississippi River fur trade to any and all comers.

Thomas L. McKenney—who directed the Factory System in its waning years, and was its biggest proponent—never faltered in his support, writing that "The system was one of pure humanity, embracing a supply of the wants of the Indians without reference to profit." But, if the Factory System had ever been memorialized with an epitaph, the following words by Secretary of War John C. Calhoun would have been the most appropriate.

> [The Factory System] was commenced, and has been continued, from motives both of prudence and humanity; and though it may not have fully realized the expectations of its friends, it has no doubt produced beneficial effects. If wars have not been entirely prevented by it, they probably, without it, would have been more frequent; and if the Indians have made but little advances in civilization, they probably, without it, would have made less.

The United States government's first experiment with nationalism failed miserably, but who knows what the outcome of the upper Missouri River and Rocky Mountain fur trade might have been had private companies and free trappers not been allowed to take the lead in opening the vast Western trade to private enterprise and entrepreneurship?

MATHILDA TAYLOR BEASLEY

[C. 1832–1903]

Mathilda Taylor Beasley, who became a nun in middle age and organized the first assembly of black nuns in the state of Georgia, was born in New Orleans, Louisiana, the daughter of a French-Creole woman (possibly a slave) and the mother's owner, James C. Taylor. Little is known about Mathilda's early childhood, but when she was little more than a teenager, and for unknown reasons, she moved to Savannah. Despite both City of Savannah and State of Georgia laws that forbade the schooling of black children by either black or white teachers, the young woman secretly opened the doors of her home to the uneducated masses of the city's black youth. Punishment of black teachers for the violation of these harsh laws was serious: a public lashing in the town square and a $100 fine.

Mathilda pursued illegally teaching for about ten years before going to work at the Railroad House, an eatery owned and operated by a black free man named Abraham Beasley, who also conducted other businesses, including running a saloon and dealing in slaves. Abraham and Mathilda married in 1869, and when Abraham died less than a decade later, he left his widow financially secure. She chose to donate all of her inheritance to the Catholic Church, traveling to England where she trained as a Franciscan nun and took her vows.

Returning to Savannah in 1887, she established the St. Francis Home for Colored Orphans. Two years later, she organized a group of black nuns associated with the Third Order of St. Francis, and soon became known as Mother Mathilda, and later, Mother Beasley. She dutifully performed her work until the day she died, December 20, 1903. She was buried in the Catholic Cemetery on Wheaton Street in Savannah. At the time, a reporter for the *Savannah Morning News* wrote, "Protestants speak in the highest terms of her life and character, and among the negroes the feeling prevails that they have lost their best and truest friend and benefactor." A municipal park located on East Broad Street is named after Mother Beasley, who was inducted into the Georgia Women's Hall of Fame in 2004.

1811

Fracas with the French

The evening of November 13, 1811, was quickly drawing to an end when several French sailors decided to leave a Savannah bawdy house and return to their ships docked at the nearby wharf. One of the ships, the *Vengeance*, had been moored in Savannah for nearly three months undergoing repairs, and most of the crew was more than familiar with the city's taverns and houses of ill repute. With nothing more to do with their time, many of the seamen spent it, as well as most of their money, at the grog shops and with the ladies of the night.

As the French privateers left the building and slowly made their way down a dark alleyway, they were met by four American seamen walking up the thoroughfare toward the bawdy house to seek their own pleasure. Precisely what happened next has become lost to history, but words were exchanged, tempers flared, weapons were drawn, and within the next few moments, one of the Americans was killed.

The next morning when news of the incident circulated around Savannah, the townspeople were aghast. How could this have happened? The French were supposed to be America's allies against Great Britain. Why would French nationals and Americans fight among themselves when they were all supposed to be friends of one another? Before any answers became apparent, another fracas got under way and another American seaman was killed by a French seaman. Savannah law enforcement officials quickly moved in and quarantined the two French ships until their crewmen could be interrogated.

Twenty-four hours of quiet followed the second killing. The men whom authorities considered to be the ringleaders of the recent violence were detained, but the rest of the French crew was released to return to their ships. In the meantime, during the early afternoon of November 15, several Savannah residents gathered at the wharf near the mooring slips of the *Vengeance* and the other French sailing ship, the *Franchise*, "with a view of offering violence to them of some description," according to a contemporary source.

None of the Georgians was in a particularly peaceable mood, and when a nervous French crewman aboard the *Franchise* saw that the mob was becoming increasingly unfriendly, he fired upon the townspeople gathered on the wharf. Retaliation was quick to follow. Within a few minutes, two French sailors were killed, several others were wounded, and the *Franchise* was commandeered by the angry Americans. Despite the efforts of the local Savannah militia to save the *Franchise* from destruction, it was set ablaze and burned down to the waterline.

In the meantime, the *Vengeance* had slipped her moorings and drifted slowly down the Savannah River toward the sea, with a full crew on board. The ship was soon captured, however, hauled back to dock, and after all aboard were arrested, the ship was set ablaze. One of the city's newspapers, the *Columbian Museum & Savannah Advertiser*, exclaimed, "We sincerely hope that the Peace of the City will not again be disturbed and that such wretches, as composed the crews of the Privateers, will not be allowed an opportunity of again shedding our citizens Blood."

The French ambassador in Washington soon became involved in the affair, as did President James Madison and Secretary of State James Monroe. The ambassador had received news that the entire situation was the work of the Americans and that his French countrymen were totally innocent of any wrongdoing. Secretary Monroe, attempting to get to the bottom of the matter, vowed that, if this were the case, the Americans responsible for the incident would be brought to justice. In the meantime, he instructed the American minister in Paris to inform the French government that, regardless of which side started the fracas, the unfortunate affair was but one of the "embarrassing consequences which results from the French Privateers hovering on our Coast, committing depradations [*sic*] on our Commerce even in the neighbourhood and then entering into our Ports."

Actually, both President Madison and Secretary of State Monroe were trying hard not to offend the French government since the United States wanted France to be an ally in the growing tensions between the United States and Great Britain. War clouds were already on the horizon, and only eight months prior to the Savannah incident, a "war-hawk" Congress had been seated that demanded the United States go to war with England.

One of the primary reasons for the ill feelings between the United States and Great Britain was the British Navy's impressment of American seamen. For several years, the British Navy had experienced a heavy loss of its own sailors through desertion. In order to partly solve the problem, authorities in London had initiated a policy of searching American vessels on the high seas for runaway sailors. The American government protested this action, especially since the British reclaimed not only their own men, but in some cases forcibly kidnapped American subjects as well. As early as 1807, the impressment problem had become such an issue that at one point the United States Congress was on the verge of declaring war, but instead imposed a trade embargo on American shipping.

In his war message on June 1, 1812, President Madison spelled out exactly wherein America's problems with Great Britain lay:

> British cruisers have been in the continued practice of violating the American flag on the great highway of nations, and of seizing and carrying off persons sailing under it, not in the exercise of a belligerent right founded on the law of nations against an enemy, but of a municipal prerogative over British subjects. . . . British cruisers have been in the practice of violating the rights and the peace of our coasts. They hover

over and harass our entering and departing commerce. To the most insulting pretensions they have added the most lawless proceedings in our very harbors, and have wantonly spilt American blood within the sanctuary of our territorial jurisdiction.

With the president and the secretary of state knowing full well that war with Great Britain was imminent—and that it was essential for France to take part in any conflict as America's ally—it is no surprise that the Savannah incident was more or less swept under the carpet. All official reference to it vanished, and even today, despite the loss of several lives and the destruction of two French ships, reference to the affair has all but disappeared outside of specialized history books. In retrospect, however, if the pursuit of the issue had been intensified—thereby further jeopardizing relations between the United States and France—it is possible that President Madison would have found himself declaring what became known as the War of 1812 on two countries instead of only one.

1829–1835

From the Great Georgia Gold Rush to the Treaty of New Echota

Within a half-century following US independence in 1776—and well before the California Gold Rush of 1849, or the Pike's Peak rush ten years later, or the several Montana gold strikes during the 1860s sent thousands of prospectors to the far West—hardy and hopeful prospectors and miners were taking gold ore from the rapid-moving mountain streams and rocky outcrops of the Southern Appalachian Mountains. The yellow metal was one of the primary reasons that Spanish, French, English, and Portuguese royalty, centuries earlier, had dispatched dozens of explorers and adventurers to the New World. Over scores of years, native empires fell and countless Indians were slaughtered because of the foreigners' lust for gold. Over hundreds of years, tons of the precious metal were either gifted to the newcomers by friendly natives, or else taken from the Indians by brute force.

Although gold was found from Alabama to Nova Scotia in and along the mountain waterways and on the eastern slopes and valleys of the Appalachians, the region that yielded the highest results encompassed the southern reaches of the mountains from Virginia southward. Although Georgia is sometimes reported to have been the home of the first gold rush in the United States, the strike that claims that honor occurred in Cabarrus County, North Carolina, in 1799. The discovery of the 17-pound nugget caused little excitement, however, since the family failed to realize it was actually gold, and used the massive lump as a doorstop.

Three years later, when the rock was certified as gold, landowners in western North Carolina began looking for—and finding—gold with increasing frequency. The finds were usually "placer" gold, which had detached itself from the quartz found along the ridges and tumbled into the gravel of stream beds.

In 1825 in North Carolina, rich veins of the gold-bearing quartz itself were discovered for the first time, opening up new and more-plentiful opportunities to find gold. Eventually an entire region of the southern mountains extending from Alabama through Georgia and the Carolinas and into Virginia was declared to be the area richest in gold. Historian and writer David Williams, in his book *The Georgia Gold Rush*, states, "One newspaper editor commented in 1829 that discoveries of gold had become so frequent that they were no longer of interest to his readers. He was sure that gold would become as common as lead. Such reports attracted thousands of miners to the Southern gold region, giving rise to America's first major gold rush."

In Georgia, the state in the gold region with the heaviest occurrence of the mineral, the first documented discovery of gold was made in the summer of 1829, although no doubt many incidental findings of the metal had been made earlier. On August 1, the *Georgia Journal* newspaper in Milledgeville announced that two gold mines had opened in the region, thus confirming "what we long anticipated . . . that the gold region of North and South Carolina would be found to extend into Georgia."

From that point forward, Georgia newspapers began reporting the progress of gold discoveries in earnest. By the following year, some sources estimated that around ten thousand gold seekers—they called themselves "twenty-niners"—were working the diggings in Georgia, most of the mining being performed on land that still belonged to the Cherokee Indians. One region particularly rich in gold was organized into Lumpkin County in 1832. The following year, a new town that became known as Dahlonega was established as the county seat while a crowd of cheering onlookers toasted, "Conceived in sin, brought forth in iniquity, cradled in corruption and located upon destruction." The US government soon established a mint in the rapidly growing boomtown that would process gold coins valued at $6 million before closing in 1861.

The 1829 gold strike coincided with the appearance in Washington, DC, of a new president, Andrew Jackson, whose dismal views on the status and "place" of Indians in America were already universally known. The combination of Jackson as president and the presence of a full-fledged gold rush, bringing in thousands of aggressive and determined miners with their sights set on getting rich, made the year a defining one for the Cherokees, and bode nothing but ill tidings.

Beginning as early as 1721, under colonial administrators, the Cherokees had already been stripped of one parcel after another of their Georgia homeland. When the torch of government passed to the infant United States, the real estate grab continued until, by the time of the gold rush, the only holding the tribe maintained was the northwest corner of the state.

Three years earlier, the Georgia senate had petitioned President John Quincy Adams to "extinguish the title to all or any part of [Cherokee] lands now in their possession within the limits of Georgia." When President Jackson orchestrated the Removal Act of 1830, many Georgians were elated to learn that the power of the federal government would now be on their side. Although the discovery of significant amounts of gold throughout a sizable portion of North Georgia certainly strengthened the state's—and the people's—arguments justifying the displacement of the Cherokees at the earliest opportunity, a successful removal mechanism clearly had already been in the works for a long time prior.

As tensions mounted within the Cherokees over their future, the tribal leadership fell into discord. One faction, the majority group led by Chief John Ross, stood adamantly against removal regardless of the consequences. The other group, called the Treaty Party, was represented by Major Ridge; his son, John Ridge; Elias Boudinot; and Stand Watie. Its followers feared that further resistance to federal demands for removal would result in the total decimation of the Cherokee Nation.

In December 1835, while John Ross was in Washington, DC, negotiating yet again with the federal government in an attempt to delay the inevitable removal, Major Ridge, his cohorts, and three hundred members of the Treaty Party met at New Echota in North Georgia to hammer out a new treaty for removal to the trans-Mississippi West, in exchange for $5 million. The treaty was signed by several delegates of the Treaty Party, none of whom were authorized by either the Cherokee Council or Chief John Ross.

The hottest temperature ever recorded in Georgia was 112 degrees Fahrenheit on July 24, 1952, at Louisville.

Needless to say, the anti-Removal faction soundly refused to support the treaty. The federal government was quick to accept it nonetheless, adding a stern warning that if removal to the West was not consummated within two years of the treaty's ratification, US Army troops would forcibly remove any Cherokees remaining east of the Mississippi River. The Removal became known as the Trail of Tears.

Ralph Waldo Emerson was one of nineteenth-century America's most respected poets and philosophers. In April 1838, a little over a year after Martin Van Buren had assumed the presidency as successor to Andrew Jackson, Emerson laid bare his emotions over Indian Removal and the federal government's hostile—and illegal—policy toward the Cherokees, thoughts which were shared by many Americans in the North and the South. About half of the epistle— the part concerning Emerson's reflections on the Treaty of New Echota and the subsequent preparations for the forced removal of the Cherokees from the entire region lying east of the Mississippi River—is reproduced here as a poignant reminder of the sensitivities of many white Americans on the other side of the nation's "Indian problem."

April 23, 1838

Sir:

The seat you fill places you in a relation of credit and nearness to every citizen. By right and natural position, every citizen is your friend. Before any acts contrary to his own judgment or interest have repelled the affections of any man, each may look with trust and living anticipation to your government. . . . Sir, my communication respects the sinister rumors that fill this part of the country concerning the Cherokee people. . . . The newspapers . . . inform us that, in December, 1835, a treaty contracting for the exchange of all the Cherokee territory was pretended to be made by an agent on the part of the United States with some persons appearing on the part of the Cherokees; that the fact afterwards transpired that these deputies did by no means represent the will of the nation; and that, out of eighteen thousand souls composing the nation, fifteen thousand six hundred and sixty-eight have protested against the so-called treaty.

It now appears that the government of the United States choose[s] to hold the Cherokees to this sham treaty, and are proceeding to execute the same. Almost the entire Cherokee Nation stand[s] up [to] say, "This is not our act. Behold us. Here are we. Do not mistake that handful of deserters for us"; and the American President and the Cabinet, the Senate and the House of Representatives, neither hear these men nor see them, and are contracting to put this active nation into carts and boats, and to drag them over mountains and rivers to a wilderness at a vast distance beyond the Mississippi. . . .

In the name of God, sir, we ask you if this be so. Do the newspapers rightly inform us? . . . We are slow to believe it. We hoped the Indians were misinformed, and that their remonstrance was premature, and will turn out to be a needless act of terror. . . . Such a dereliction of all faith and virtue, such a denial of justice, and such deafness to screams for mercy were never heard of in times of peace and in the dealing of a nation with its own allies and wards, since the earth was made. Sir, does this government think that the people of the United States are become savage and mad? From their mind are the sentiments of love and a good nature wiped clean out? The soul of man, the justice, the mercy that is the heart in all men from Maine to Georgia, does abhor this business. . . . You, sir, will bring down that renowned chair in which you sit into infamy if your seal is set to this instrument of perfidy; and the name of this nation, hitherto the sweet omen of religion and liberty, will stink to the world. You will not do us the injustice of connecting this remonstrance with any sectional and party feeling. It is in our hearts the simplest commandment of brotherly love. We will not have this great and solemn claim upon national and human justice huddled aside under the flimsy plea of its being a party act. . . .

[T]here exists in a great part of the Northern people a gloomy diffidence in the moral character of the government. On the broaching of this question, a general expression of despondency, of disbelief that any good will accrue from a remonstrance on an act of fraud and robbery. . . . Will the American government steal? Will it lie? Will it kill? . . . Our counselors and old statesmen here say that ten years ago they would have staked their lives on the affirmation that the proposed Indian measures could not be executed; that the unanimous country would put them down. And now the steps of this crime follow each other so fast, at such fatally quick time, that the millions of virtuous citizens, whose agents the government are, have no place to interpose, and must shut their eyes until the last howl and wailing of these tormented villages and tribes shall afflict the ear of the world. . . .

I write thus, sir, to inform you of the state of mind these Indian tidings have awakened . . . and to pray with one voice more that you, whose hands are strong with the delegated power of fifteen millions of men, will avert with that might the terrific injury which threatens the Cherokee tribe.

With great respect, sir, I am your fellow citizen,

Ralph Waldo Emerson

The following month, American soldiers began corralling Cherokee men, women, and children, the old and the infirm, into holding areas in Tennessee and Alabama to prepare for the trip to Indian Territory. After a grueling journey, some by riverboat and some traveling overland, the Cherokees arrived at their destination during the spring of 1839. Around four thousand died in the process. Major Ridge, John Ridge, and Elias Boudinot eventually paid the supreme price for their duplicity in orchestrating the illegal Treaty of New Echota. All three were assassinated shortly after arriving at their new home. Stand Watie escaped the carnage and lived to become a general in the Confederate Army. John Ross lost his beloved wife on the Trail of Tears and lived until 1866, leading his people into a new era in present-day Oklahoma.

REBECCA LATIMER FELTON

[1835–1930]

It is unlikely today that very many Americans—even those who consider themselves well versed in political affairs—realize that back in 1922, an eighty-seven-year-old widow and DeKalb County native became the first female to serve in the US Senate, or that she filled her post for only a single day before being replaced.

Rebecca Felton had already lived a long and interesting life by the time of her twenty-four hours of fame, but even in the twilight of her days, she was a powerful voice to be reckoned with. When she died in 1930, her life had spanned the years between the fall of the Alamo to Adolf Hitler's terrifying rise to power. Following her graduation, with honors, from nearby Madison Female College, she married William H. Felton, a widowed planter, physician, and state legislator. A score of years later, greatly assisted by Rebecca's strong will and desire for her husband's success, Felton was elected to the US Congress, where he served for three terms, followed by three terms in the Georgia legislature. Throughout Felton's political career, his faithful wife worked by his side as his campaign manager, speechwriter, public relations liaison, and more.

Upon her husband's retirement in the mid-1890s, Rebecca turned her focus upon her own career and the betterment of society. She fought for the elimination of Georgia's convict lease system, the improvement of the state's public education system, and, most especially, women's suffrage. For twenty years, she authored a regular feature in the *Atlanta Journal* devoted to rural issues. Her senatorial career began shortly after Senator Thomas E. Watson died in September of 1922 during the congressional recess. The sitting governor (and former state senator), Thomas Hardwick, was defeated by Rebecca's friend and mentor, Walter F. George, in the special election for the senate seat. However, in a move to honor Rebecca Felton's decades of service to her country—as well as to attempt to make amends to his female constituents for having voted against the Nineteenth Amendment—Hardwick had already appointed her as interim senator prior to the special election. Mrs. Felton was sworn in for her symbolic daylong reign as Georgia's first female senator before Senator George began his official term.

1838

The Trail of Tears

Winfield Scott carefully lowered his lumbering 6-foot-3-inch frame into a rickety camp chair inside his makeshift tent located amid the lush green mountains of North Georgia. Scott, a major-general and the second-highest-ranking officer in the United States Army, did not look forward to completing his most recent orders. He had only recently returned from a long campaign against the Seminole Indians deep in the sweltering swamps of Florida, and prior to that he had been passed over for a promotion to commanding general of the entire US Army. Now, on the eve of yet another controversial assignment, it seemed to the fifty-one-year-old general that he always ended up with the most undesirable and unwanted duty.

It was spring of 1838 and General Scott had been ordered to forcibly move the Cherokee tribe to lands beyond the Mississippi River. For eight years now—ever since President Andrew Jackson signed the Indian Removal Act—federal authorities had attempted to expel the fifteen thousand members of the proud Cherokee Nation from their traditional lands in Georgia, Tennessee, and North Carolina. Soon after the passage of the Removal Act, the tribe's chief, John Ross, had avoided the inevitable by taking the United States government to court on the grounds that the Removal Act was illegal. When the Cherokees won their case in the United States Supreme Court in 1831, President Jackson's response had been, "John Marshall [the court's chief justice] has made his decision. Now let him enforce it."

To complicate matters, Major John Ridge, who aspired to become chief of the Cherokee Nation, had signed a treaty in 1835 at New Echota, Georgia, that relinquished all remaining Cherokee lands east of the Mississippi River to the government. Questions were immediately raised as to the treaty's legality since only a small segment of the Cherokee leadership had approved it. Nevertheless, federal officials pointed to the controversial document as their authority to demand the Cherokees' expulsion.

Now, time had nearly run out for John Ross and his stalwart followers who had no desire to relocate beyond the Mississippi River. General Scott and seven thousand troops had recently arrived in Cherokee country to see that the government's will was carried out. Stockades had been built to house the Cherokees after they were forced to leave their homes and farmsteads, and supplies—one pound of flour and a half-pound of bacon daily for each Cherokee—had been gathered to distribute among the disheartened Indians.

General Scott carefully pulled a letter from a packet of documents, mindfully unfolded it, and once again read his controversial orders.

> From recent intelligence received from the Government agents among the Cherokees, it is apprehended that the mass of the nation, under some delusion, does not intend to remove to the country provided for them under the stipulations of the treaty.... You will, therefore, repair, without unnecessary delay, to Athens, in Tennessee, or to any other point in your opinion most convenient for making your arrangements. Orders have been given for the 4th regiment of artillery, the 4th regiment of infantry, and six companies of the 2d dragoons, now in Florida, to repair, as early as practicable, to the Cherokee country.... You are authorized to call on the Governors of the States of Tennessee, North Carolina, Georgia, and Alabama, for such militia and volunteer force, not exceeding 4,000, in addition to the regular forces, as you may deem necessary.

Scott closed his eyes, thought for a moment, then reached across his field desk and plucked the feathered quill pen from its inkwell. Smoothing a long piece of yellowed paper on the rough surface of the desk, the troubled general began to write.

> Cherokees! The President of the United States has sent me with a powerful army, to cause you, in obedience to the treaty of 1835, to join that part of your people who are already established in prosperity on the other side of the Mississippi. Unhappily, the two years which were allowed for the purpose, you

have suffered to pass away without following, and without making any preparation to follow; and now, or by the time that this solemn address shall reach your distant settlements, the emigration must be commenced in haste, but I hope without disorder. I have no power, by granting a farther delay, to correct the error that you have committed. The full moon of May is already on the wane; and before another shall have passed away, every Cherokee man, woman, and child, in those States, must be in motion to join their brethren in the far West.

For the next several weeks, Scott oversaw the collection of thousands of Cherokees and forced them into confinement in the log stockades that had been built to receive them. He admonished his troops to treat the natives with "every possible kindness," warning them that "simple indiscretions, acts of harshness, and cruelty . . . may lead . . . to delays, to impatience, and exasperation, and in the end, to a general war and carnage." The general suggested that "by early and persevering acts of kindness and humanity, it is impossible to doubt that the Indians may soon be induced to confide in the army, and, instead of fleeing to mountains and forest, flock to us for food and clothing."

By summer the long migration of thousands of Cherokees to the new land had begun. Two routes were used: One followed the river system down the Tennessee, Ohio, and Mississippi to the mouth of the Arkansas and up that stream to present-day Oklahoma. In October, an overland party started on a second route and trekked through Nashville, across Kentucky and part of southern Illinois, ferried over the Mississippi River into Missouri, and marched thence to

Oklahoma. Finally, the last group to leave the ancient Cherokee homeland—including John Ross, his wife, and those too sick to travel overland—left Ross's Landing on boat to travel down the Tennessee River. The entire forced migration became known as the Trail of Tears. About four thousand of the fourteen thousand Indians who traveled the Trail of Tears died along the trail, including John Ross's wife. Ross himself went on to become a diligent worker for his people in their new homeland, eventually becoming principal chief of the western branch of the tribe.

A few hundred Cherokees in Georgia escaped the watchful eye of the army and took refuge in the dense forests of the Southern Appalachians. Their descendants still live there today.

1842

The First Surgical Use of Ether

During the evening of March 30, 1842, an unseasonably cool breezy day in Jefferson, Georgia, five men gathered in a first floor room of Dr. Crawford Long's two-story office building located on College Street. Present, in addition to Dr. Long himself, were James M. Venable, Edmund S. Rawls, and brothers Andrew J. and William H. Thurmond. Twenty-six-year-old Long placed James Venable in a chair close to the room's front window in order to capture as much light as possible from the rapidly fading sun.

Rawls and the Thurmond brothers watched as Dr. Long ordered Venable to remove his shirt. The physician then swabbed the back of Venable's neck with alcohol and allowed the spot to air dry. Next, Dr. Long took a neatly folded towel and poured a strong-smelling concoction called ether onto it, crumpled it up to make sure the liquid had saturated it, and quickly placed the cloth over Venable's nose and mouth. After the young Jefferson Academy student took a few deep breaths, he fell into a deep sleep.

Dr. Long now moved rapidly. With a scalpel, he deftly cut into the back of Venable's neck and, within a few brief minutes, had removed a small, one-half-inch tumor from the site. Midway through the operation, he poured more ether on the towel to assure that Venable would stay unconscious during the entire surgical procedure. A few years later, recalling this momentous event, Dr. Long wrote:

> The patient continued to inhale ether during the time of the operation; and when informed it was over, seemed incredulous, until the tumour was shown him. He gave no evidence of suffering during the operation, and assured me, after it was over, that he did not experience the slightest degree of pain from its performance.

Dr. Long's excision of James Venable's tumor on that day long ago in 1842 in Jefferson, Georgia, denotes the discovery and first practical use of anesthesia. Previously, whenever surgery was performed upon a patient, he had to endure the procedure while wide awake, with no means of alleviating the excruciating pain that accompanied it.

On June 6, 1842, Dr. Long removed a second tumor from James Venable's neck. Of this more complicated procedure, Long wrote:

> This operation required more time than the first, from the cyst of the tumour having formed adhesions to the surrounding parts. The patient was

insensible to pain during the operation, until the last attachment of the cyst was separated, when he exhibited signs of slight suffering but asserted, after the operation was over, that the sensation of pain was so slight as scarcely to be perceived. In this operation the inhalation of ether ceased before the first incision was made; since that time I have invariably desired patients when practicable, to continue its inhalation during the time of the operation.

Dr. Long performed one more surgery using ether during 1842. On that occasion, which took place on July 3, he amputated a toe from the foot of a slave boy who lived on a plantation located about 9 miles out of town. The slave's owner, Mrs. Sabrey Hemphill, confirmed that the surgery was painless when she later wrote:

I sent my negro boy, Jack, to Dr. C. W. Long to have his toe examined and cut off if necessary. The boy was sent some time during the summer and on the Sabbath. After the boy returned home he informed me that Dr. Long cut off his toe and that he did not suffer any pain from the operation.

Perhaps the most amazing aspect of Dr. Long's successful experimentation with ether as an anesthetic is just how the concept entered his mind in the first place. During the early 1840s, when Dr. Long opened his medical practice in Jefferson, there were few ways for young people to spend their leisure time.

Like today's young men and women far away from home at college, Long found the time to entertain himself. In his day, the big fad going around the schools in the East was the inhalation of nitrous oxide gas, a chemical composition that provided a highly exhilarating effect upon those who sniffed it. Soon after the young doctor returned home from his studies in Philadelphia, news of the "sniffing" craze among young people reached the backcountry of Georgia, and Dr. Long and some of his new friends began to enjoy the euphoria of inhaling nitrous oxide.

Georgia became the fourth state to join the United States in 1788.

On one occasion when approached by some of his associates to provide them with nitrous oxide, Dr. Long replied that he had no facility for manufacturing the gas, but that he had experimented with a substance called ether, which gave the same effects. Long later reported:

I had inhaled it [ether] myself, and considered it as safe as the nitrous oxide gas. One of the company stated that he had inhaled ether while at school, and was then willing to inhale it. The company were all anxious to witness its effects. The ether was introduced: I gave it first to the gentleman who had previously inhaled it, then inhaled it myself, and afterwards gave it to all persons present. They were so much pleased with the exhilarating effects of ether, that they afterwards inhaled it frequently, and induced others to do so, and its inhalation soon became quite fashionable in this county, and in fact extended from this place through several counties in this part of Georgia.

Because Dr. Long did not publish the results of his successful experimentation with ether until 1849, other dentists and physicians of the time—William T. Morton or Charles T. Jackson of Boston, Massachusetts, or Horace Wells of Hartford, Connecticut—have sometimes been credited as the real discoverers of anesthesia. These men were some of the first to use ether and prove that when administered properly, it made surgery painless, but it was Dr. Crawford Long who first used the "miracle gas" that would continue to be used in nearly all surgical procedures for the next century.

1862

The Case of the Double-Barreled Cannon

On a sunny spring day in 1862, several score of townspeople from Athens, Georgia, gathered in a large, partially wooded field at nearby Linton Springs. There was a carnival atmosphere in the air, and as men, women, and children gathered together in small groups to chat about the upcoming events, all kept their eyes on John Wesley Gilleland Sr. All those present knew Old Man Gilleland. Over the years he had doctored practically everybody in the crowd. A man who loved tinkering with machinery, he had even designed prototypes for a few bizarre mechanical tools, most of which were never put into production.

The item that Gilleland was demonstrating to his neighbors that day, however, had the possibility of being very different from the others. For several weeks now, gossip had spread throughout the Athens countryside that Dr. Gilleland had invented an awesome new weapon—a magnificent, double-barreled cannon that, once mass-produced and put into operation with the Confederate artillery, would cause such fear in the Yankees that they would go back north where they came from. Some folks were saying that Gilleland's innovative cannon would shorten the Civil War by months, maybe even years!

On the day of the big demonstration, Gilleland had sent out a work crew to the field at Linton Springs to clear some of the trees along a pathway that stretched down the meadow for several hundred yards. Then, the workers hauled out the cannon and pointed it down the lane between the remaining rows of trees. Finally, at the end of the cleared land, they placed several upright poles to represent enemy soldiers.

A totally silent crowd watched as Gilleland rammed powder down the twin barrels of the cannon. Next, his two assistants walked up to the muzzles and picked up a cannon ball. But the spectators noticed something different about the missiles. They were connected together by a long chain! One ball was dropped down each barrel while the chain was left dangling between the muzzles of the barrels. By now most of the onlookers understood the concept of the cannon. For those who didn't, Dr. Gilleland explained that when the two balls simultaneously left the side-by-side barrels, they would be hurled away from each other until the chain was drawn taunt between them. Then, in the words of an early-twentieth-century historian, the balls and chain would "mow down the enemy somewhat as a scythe cuts wheat."

Dr. Gilleland cautioned the crowd to stand well away from the line of fire as he and his associates prepared for firing the cannon. When all was ready, the fuse was lit, resulting in a violent roar. One barrel's powder charge exploded a mere fraction of a second earlier than the other one, causing its ball to leave its barrel first. The second ball exited its barrel immediately afterwards. But, the velocity and weight of the first ball, by now already speeding through the air, caused the chain to break. The first ball, with the chain attached and whipping about, landed among the uncut trees, while the second missile struck, as A. L. Hull reported in his Annals of Athens, Georgia, "wide of the mark, and the poles which represented the hostile army stood uninjured."

To say the least, Dr. Gilleland was disappointed, as were all of the curious onlookers. But the inventor was not to be outdone. After his initial effort to prove that a double-barreled cannon was not only practical but that it might be the weapon to save the Confederacy, he returned home to Athens to work on the cannonball and chain design, wherein he felt the failure lay. On April 30, 1862, a local newspaper, the *Southern Watchman*, happily reported that the cannon "has been tested and found to be satisfactory!"

Gilleland's next step in getting his weapon sanctioned by the Confederate government was to take it to the arsenal at Augusta to demonstrate its abilities to the commandant, Lieutenant Colonel G. W. Rains. Rains watched as the inventor fired two successive volleys—the arsenal only had enough chain for two shots—from the cannon. Unimpressed, Rains declared that he thought the weapon was impractical.

Dr. Gilleland then contacted the Confederate secretary of war, Robert Toombs. In a letter dated March 5, 1863, Gilleland pleaded with Toombs to consider adopting the cannon for use in the army, assuring the secretary that he demonstrated his cannon "several times before an intelegant [*sic*] people and they are convinced that it is a perfect success."

Toombs ordered his ordinance chief, Colonel Josiah Gorgas to take a look at Dr. Gilleland's cannon and to give a recommendation on whether it should be adopted by the artillery. Gorgas was highly critical of the device, writing that, "It is absolutely impossible to fire off two charges of powder by any means whatever (electricity or otherwise) so that the quantities of powder that shall be burned, or the initial force evolved, shall be precisely the same at any given moment of time." The colonel concluded that this shortcoming would "cause one ball to lead the other on leaving the piece, which will either break the chain . . . by the jerk, or cause the balls to pursue a revolving course and take up an erratic and, in some cases, dangerous trajectory to persons in its vicinity."

> *Georgia was named in honor of Great Britain's King George II.*

Finally admitting defeat, the dejected Dr. Gilleland donated his cannon to the city of Athens. The weapon was placed in front of the town hall where it was used to fire warning shots in case of enemy attack. Although its exact use during the latter days of the war is unknown, it is assumed that it was fired in August 1864 to forewarn Athens citizens that Stoneman's Raiders were about to attack.

A quarter of a century after the war, Dr. Gilleland's cannon abruptly disappeared from City Hall's lawn. Some speculated that it was carted off with the debris of the building after it burned to the ground in 1893. For five years the cannon's whereabouts were unknown, then, in 1898, a young Athens boy accidentally discovered it in a rock pile in his backyard. For four dollars the boy peddled it to a junk dealer who recognized the piece and passed it on to two men who remembered when it was manufactured and tested back in 1862. The cannon eventually came back to rest on the lawn of City Hall. A Georgia Historical Commission monument was erected in 1957 to commemorate the weapon's interesting story.

TYRUS RAYMOND "TY" COBB

[1886–1961]

The website for the National Baseball Hall of Fame in Cooperstown, New York, declares that "Ty Cobb may have been the best all-around baseball player that ever lived. But one thing is for sure, Cobb had a burning desire to win."

There is no doubt that Cobb was one of the most aggressive, no-nonsense players ever to swing a bat, catch a fly, or field a grounder in major league history. The Narrows, Georgia, native once proclaimed that "I never could stand losing. Second place didn't interest me. I had a fire in my belly." He also remarked that "Baseball is a red-blooded sport for red-blooded men. It's no pink tea, and mollycoddles had better stay out. It's a struggle for supremacy, a survival of the fittest." This pretty much sums up one of baseball's most legendary—and controversial—players of all time.

Cobb began his professional career in the old South Atlantic League soon after it was organized in 1904. Shortly afterwards, he moved up to the Detroit Tigers, where he played center field for twenty-two seasons, five of them—1921 through 1926—as

player-manager, before being traded to the Philadelphia Athletics and playing for two additional years until his retirement. For his career efforts, Cobb was inducted into the National Baseball Hall of Fame in 1936 as one of five charter members, along with pitchers Walter Johnson and Christy Mathewson, right fielder Babe Ruth, and shortstop Honus Wagner.

Ty Cobb was a record-setter. During his twenty-four seasons of play, his batting average was .320 or higher for twenty-two of them, with three seasons reaching over .400. He won the American League (AL) batting title for twelve seasons. During the 1911 season, he was the AL leader in numbers of hits, runs batted in, runs scored, and batting average, and earned the most valuable player award for the AL as well.

Legendary Hall of Fame manager Casey Stengel admitted, "I never saw anyone like Ty Cobb. No one even close to him. He was the greatest all-time ballplayer. That guy was superhuman, amazing." George Sisler, another Hall of Famer, added, "To see him was to remember him forever."

1862

The Great Locomotive Chase

Thick black smoke poured from the smokestack of the *General*, the state-of-the-art locomotive that was the pride and joy of the Western & Atlantic Railroad Company. Capable of running almost one mile per minute, the *General* pulled a short train made up of a wood tender, three empty box cars, and several passenger coaches. It was Saturday morning, April 12, 1862, and the train had left Atlanta at 6:00 a.m., northbound for Chattanooga, Tennessee, some 130 miles away.

There was a great deal of excitement onboard the train that morning. News had just been received in Atlanta that Confederate-held Fort Pulaski, a massive coastal defense post located outside Savannah, had fallen after a long blistering Union bombardment the day before. With Fort Pulaski now in enemy hands, the southeastern approach to Atlanta was exposed, placing the city in danger of being invaded from that direction. And to add to the bad news, the train passengers also learned that Union General Ormsby Mitchel had occupied the town of Huntsville, Alabama, situated only a few miles west of Confederate-occupied Chattanooga. A week before the Confederate army had been defeated at the battle of Shiloh, in Tennessee, and it suddenly appeared— even more so now with the occupation of Huntsville—that the heart of the Southland, the strategic corridor stretching between Nashville and Atlanta, might soon be in Union hands.

When the *General* pulled into the depot at Marietta, a station just a few miles north of Atlanta, twenty men dressed in civilian clothes boarded the train and took seats at various places in the passenger coaches. To the Georgians riding the train that morning, the men looked and acted like all the rest of the riders. In retrospect, however, some noticed that most of the newcomers did little talking among themselves, almost as if their minds were preoccupied with some overwhelming mission. Indeed, the men did have an unusual mission— these plain-clothed Union soldiers were raiders planning to steal the *General*, head off toward Chattanooga and General Mitchel, and destroy as much Western & Atlantic railroad property as they could.

The men had barely settled in their seats when the conductor announced that the train would make a twenty-minute breakfast stop at the upcoming station, Big Shanty, today's village of Kennesaw. After the *General* came to a halt at the depot and hotel at Big Shanty, most of the Atlanta passengers, as well as the entire crew, rapidly left the train and headed for breakfast. No one noticed the activities of the raiders. While one uncoupled the passenger cars from the rest of the train, the group's leader, Captain James J. Andrews, quickly hustled sixteen of his companions into the train's empty box cars. Andrews and the three remaining men then boarded the engine, brought the *General* to a full head of steam, and started northward toward the next town.

One of the raiders accidentally rang the locomotive's bell as the *General* and its lightened load pulled out of Big Shanty, alarming the crew inside the hotel, as well as many of the three thousand Confederate soldiers encamped nearby. The locomotive's engineer, Jeff Cain, and the train's conductor, William A. Fuller, reached the loading platform to see the train nearly out of sight around a bend. Since Big Shanty was not equipped with a telegraph, quick-witted Anthony Murphy, a master mechanic for the Western & Atlantic railroad line, swiftly dispatched a horseman to the telegraph station in Marietta to get the news of the theft of the train on the wires as rapidly as possible. However, Captain Andrews had already stopped the *General* a few miles out of Big Shanty and cut the telegraph lines.

In the meantime, the athletic Fuller, just three days short of his twenty-sixth birthday, lit out on foot after the rapidly escaping train. After running at top speed for nearly 3 miles,

he reached the tiny community of Moon's Station. A track repair team there reported that the stolen train had just passed by, and its riders had commandeered most of the workers' tools. Fuller pushed a hand car back down the tracks to Big Shanty, picked up Cain and

Murphy, and then traveled the dozen or so miles to the next stop at Etowah where they found another locomotive, the *Yonah*, waiting with a full head of steam.

From Etowah, on board the *Yonah*, Fuller and his followers sped 14 miles to Kingston. At Kingston, Fuller discovered several trains stalled along the tracks. He was told that Captain Andrews had been delayed there for an hour due to the heavy volume on the tracks, but he had eventually persuaded all of the trains' engineers to pull onto the sidings by telling them that he was carrying precious supplies for the Confederacy.

Fuller now switched engines, commandeering one belonging to the rival Rome Railroad. Leaving town only minutes after Andrews, Fuller soon ran into several lengths of rails that had been purposely damaged by Andrews and his men in order to hinder their pursuers. Unable to get his engine past the rail damage, Fuller and some of his men again took off on foot until they met a southbound freight train pulled by the locomotive *Texas*. Fuller quickly explained the situation to the engineer of the Texas, uncoupled all of the box cars, and commenced to run the engine backwards up the tracks in pursuit of the *General*.

Fuller, driving full speed in the *Texas*, pursued Andrews and the *General* for several miles. Andrews stopped his train at every opportunity for his men to destroy track, dump ties across the rails, and cut telegraph wires; efforts to burn several railroad bridges, however, were hindered when Andrews discovered that the bridge timbers were soaking wet from recent heavy rains. Meanwhile, Fuller made such good time on his chase that at one point on the wild ride, the *Texas* almost reached the *General*.

As Andrews approached the town of Ringgold, Georgia, located a few miles south of the Tennessee border, he lost all hope of ever accomplishing his mission. He had no more wood to feed the *General*'s hungry boilers, and he knew that the local militia had been alerted to be on the lookout for his command. He finally instructed his men to desert the train, flee into the woods, and "escape the best you can." Andrews and his followers were eventually caught and tried. Eight of them, Andrews included, were executed in Atlanta as spies.

The Andrews Raid, as this episode in Georgia history is known, was a failure as far as the Union command was concerned, because the Western & Atlantic railroad line was restored to full working order within a few days. The participants in the raid—all of whom, except for Andrews and one other, were members of the Second, Twenty-first, and Thirty-third Ohio Volunteer Infantry—received the first Medals of Honor ever presented by the US Congress to American fighting men.

1864

Roswell Factory Workers Deported

As the hot days of July 1864 dragged on and practically every moment brought another rumor that the Union army was rapidly approaching Atlanta, four hundred young women and girls kept themselves busy working in the civilian textile mill in nearby Roswell. When Confederate general Joseph E. Johnston fell back toward the Chattahoochee River with his Army of Tennessee, the mill was left unprotected, and Union General Kenner Garrard's Second Cavalry Division quickly seized the opportunity, on the night of July 6, to burn the factory to the ground.

Before the flames had subsided, Garrard reported to his superior, General William Tecumseh Sherman, that the mill was flying a French flag. Adding that he torched the mill, he continued, saying, "The cotton factory was worked up to the

time of its destruction, some 400 women being employed."
The following day, Sherman replied to Garrard:

> ... arrest the owners and the employees and send
> them, under guard, charged [with] hoisting the
> French flag and then devoting his labor and capital
> with treason, to Marietta and I will see as to any man
> in America in supplying armies in open hostility to
> our Government and then claiming the benefit of his
> neutral flag. Should you under the impulse of anger,
> natural or contemplating such perfidy, hang the
> wretch I approve.

Several suggestions have been forwarded as to why a
French flag flew over the Roswell mill on July 6, 1864, but
the most logical explanation is that a frightened employee
simply ran up the banner hoping that the aggressive Union
troops would leave the mill and its workers unharmed. Whatever the intent was, the ploy failed to impress Garrard's men
as they destroyed every building in sight.

Georgia contains 159 counties.

General Sherman ordered Garrard to "arrest all people,
male and female, connected with those factories, no matter
what the clamor and let them foot it, under guard, to Marietta,
whence I will send them by cars to the North" and promised
"to get rid of them here." Several accounts exist regarding
the methods used to move the women 13 miles to Marietta.
Some say that each cavalryman carried a female behind him
on his horse, while others report that all the workers were

transported by wagons. The latter theory seems to be confirmed by a reporter for the *New York Tribune* who sarcastically wrote:

> Only think of it! Four hundred weeping and terrified Ellens, Susans, and Maggies transported in the seatless and springless army wagons, away from their lovers and brothers of the sunny South; and all this for the offense of weaving tent cloth and spinning stocking yarn!

Regardless of how they were moved, all of the terrified and homeless women and girls arrived in Marietta by July 10. The next few hours for them were horrible as they wondered what fates awaited them. Some of them did not have to wait long. A sergeant in General Garrard's cavalry division wrote:

> The employees were all women and there were more of them than we had seen since leaving Nashville . . . [they] were really good looking; most of the women we have seen for the past year have been fearfully homely. . . . According to promise, Gen. Garrard right away after breakfast this morning, sent around the whiskey. This was the second time we ever had drawn, or ever had, whiskey issued to us since we entered the service and we think "this" was a mistake, as the men never needed it or asked for it, and always got along just as well without it. The whiskey ration was about a gill, and not enough to hurt anyone, provided each one just drank his own ration; but there were always in each company some who would never draw their rations at all, which would leave just that much for somebody else, while among

those who did draw their rations, there were some who were not content to drink them alone, but had a way of gambling "drink for drink" till some would get a pint, or even a quart, and of course get foolishly drunk. Upon this occasion their delirium took the form of making love to the women, and before night, Col. Miller found it necessary to move the brigade a mile north of the town.

For the next two days, the women were housed in Marietta while they pondered their fate. Then, they were packed into box cars and shipped north to federal headquarters in Nashville. Their journey continued to the Ohio River and beyond. By July 21, the factory workers, nearly two hundred and fifty of them, arrived in New Albany, Indiana, situated across the Ohio from Louisville. Journalists for many of the northern newspapers agreed with General Sherman's harsh treatment of the displaced women, but at least one newspaperman, the editor of the *New York Commercial Advertiser*, wrote a scathing indictment of Sherman and his policies:

> . . . it is hardly conceivable that an officer bearing a United States commission of Major General should have so far forgotten the commonest dictates of decency and humanity . . . as to drive four hundred penniless girls hundreds of miles away from their homes and friends to seek their livelihood amid strange and hostile people. We repeat our earnest hope that further information may redeem the name of General Sherman and our own from the frightful disgrace which this story as it now comes to us must else inflict upon one and the other.

Although history does not reveal what happened to the majority of the women and girls who were taken from their homeland to a strange country, at least one newspaper account states that some of them made their way back to Georgia after the Civil War, while others stayed in their new homes, eventually married and raised families. An 1896 issue of the *Confederate Veteran* magazine painted a far bleaker picture for the deportees, however, when it reported that "all women were scattered to the four winds. Very few if any of these poor women ever saw their native soil again."

ERSKINE CALDWELL

(1903–1987)

Erskine Caldwell was one of America's most influential writers of the mid-twentieth century. He was born an only child in Coweta County, Georgia, but as a youngster moved throughout much of the South with his schoolteacher mother and preacher-father. Upon the family's return to Georgia, they settled in the small village of Wrens, population about one thousand, located a few miles southwest of Augusta. After high school, Caldwell attended Erskine College in South Carolina, then the University of Virginia (UVA). Although he did not graduate from UVA, he did get his first taste of writing success there when his essay, "The Georgia Crackers," was published in 1926, followed by other pieces of short fiction in various small literary magazines. When Charles Scribner's Sons' iconic editor Maxwell Perkins took F. Scott Fitzgerald's advice and gave serious consideration to some of Caldwell's writings, the rest, as they say, is history.

Caldwell's collection of short Southern fiction entitled *American Earth* was published by Perkins in 1931, rapidly followed by *Tobacco Road* in 1932 and *God's Little Acre* in 1933.

The bestsellers depict harsh life in the rural South during the Depression as it affected white tenant farmers (*Tobacco Road*), and "the abuse of [S]outhern industrial workers and the disintegration of a family" (*God's Little Acre*).

Tobacco Road was adapted for the stage in 1933 and ran for eight years, becoming the second-longest-running Broadway play. A film adaptation, with comedic overtones, was released by Hollywood in 1941. *Tobacco Road*, the book—arguably Caldwell's finest fictional work—is among Modern Library's best one hundred novels.

In 1937, Caldwell turned to nonfiction and, collaborating with the celebrated photographer Margaret Bourke-White, produced *You Have Seen Their Faces*, a collection of photographs and interviews with people across the South about their experiences and challenges during the Depression. The experience resulted in Caldwell and Bourke-White getting married, but their union ended after only three years. Caldwell's last book, an autobiography, was published one month before his death.

1864

From Atlanta to the Sea

Thursday, September 1, 1864, was an ominous day for Georgians in general and Atlantans in particular. After weeks of Union and Confederate skirmishing in the region between Chattanooga and Atlanta, the United States Army, under the command of General William Tecumseh Sherman, had finally prevailed. The occupation of Atlanta appeared to be only hours away. General John Bell Hood ordered his Confederates to immediately evacuate the city, and the long columns of soldiers began to depart during the late afternoon. Hood also ordered southern railroad equipment as well as a large quantity of arms and ammunition too burdensome to carry to be destroyed along with the depot. Realizing that Atlanta was no longer his, Hood now had only two goals in mind—to protect the Army of Tennessee and to see his men fight again.

The following day while Hood's retreating army marched toward the community of Lovejoy's Station, situated a few miles south of Atlanta, soldiers in General Sherman's victorious army, under the command of General H. W. Slocum, entered Atlanta. Sherman, in pursuit of Hood, proudly telegraphed war department officials in Washington that the city had been "fairly won." Thrilled by Sherman's victory, President Abraham Lincoln declared September 5, 1864, a national day of celebration.

On Wednesday, September 7, General Sherman sat down at his headquarters and wrote an official dispatch to General Hood. "I have deemed it to the best interest of the United States that the citizens now residing in Atlanta should remove, those who prefer it to go South and the rest North," he declared. Continuing, he curtly wrote, "If the people raise a howl against my barbarity and cruelty, I will answer that war is war and not popularity-seeking." During the next ten days, more than sixteen hundred out of almost ten thousand terrified Atlanta residents packed up what few personal articles they could carry with them, turned their backs on their homes and everything else they owned, and evacuated the city.

Sherman was proud of his success, as were most of the Northern newspapers. The editor of one of them called Sherman's tactics a "brilliant strategic movement," while Sherman himself wrote, "The rebels have lost, beside the important city of Atlanta and stores, at least five hundred dead, two thousand five hundred wounded, and three thousand prisoners. . . . If that is not success I don't know what is."

For the next several weeks, desultory fighting continued around Atlanta. General Hood launched a major attempt to cut Sherman's supply lines from Chattanooga, and despite limited success, he and his Army of Tennessee eventually turned west and marched into Alabama, poised for reentry into Tennessee. In the meantime, General Sherman's army had been resting and re-arming in Atlanta, readying themselves for a move that was anticipated but about which little was known. It was Sherman's secret, and few knew that the general was planning a massive march from Atlanta to Savannah, and, if necessary, the destruction of everything that stood in his way.

On November 8, Sherman broke the news from his headquarters in Kingston, Georgia, located a few miles north of Atlanta. Although he still did not reveal his army's final destination, he wrote that he deemed it "proper at this time to inform the officers and men of the Fourteenth, Fifteenth, Seventeenth, and Twentieth Corps, that he has organized them into an army for a special purpose, well known to the War Department from our present base, and a long and difficult march to a new one."

Additional orders released by Sherman the following day disclosed that the army would be divided between a right and a left wing, commanded by Generals Oliver O. Howard and H. W. Slocum, respectively. General ammunition or supply trains would not accompany the army, but rather each brigade would be followed by its own ammunition wagons and ambulances, bringing up the rear of each regiment. Each column was specifically ordered to begin its march promptly at seven o'clock in the morning and to travel 15 miles per day.

Little food and other provisions were brought along, and Sherman addressed the problem as follows:

> The army will forage liberally on the country during the march. To this end, each brigade commander

will organize a good and sufficient foraging party, under the command of one or more discreet officers, who will gather, near the route traveled, corn or forage of any kind, meat of any kind, vegetables, cornmeal, or whatever is needed by the command, aiming at all times to keep in the wagons at least ten days' provisions for his command, and three days' forage. Soldiers must not enter the dwellings of inhabitants, or commit any trespass; but, during a halt or camp, they may be permitted to gather turnips, potatoes, and other vegetables, and to drive in stock in sight of their camp.

Sherman made it clear in his orders that horses, mules, and wagons that belonged to private citizens along the march could be confiscated "freely and without limit." He gave corps commanders the authority to "destroy mills, houses, cotton-gins, etc.," but warned that "In districts and neighborhoods where the army is unmolested, no destruction of such property should be permitted." However, he added "should the inhabitants burn bridges obstruct roads, or otherwise manifest local hostility, then army commanders should order and enforce a devastation more or less relentless."

Sherman was intent on making his march to the sea successful and visualized that when his march was finished the South would have been brought to its knees. He was not interested in receiving countermanding orders from anyone—not General Ulysses S. Grant, not even President Lincoln. To avoid contact with army headquarters during this radical campaign, and to assure that his plan was not overturned, Sherman had his men cut all telegraph wires, thus placing his command in total isolation.

On December 6, 1864, four days before Sherman marched into Savannah, General Grant finally tracked him down and wrote to him saying, "You have now destroyed the roads of the South so that it will probably take them three months without interruption to reestablish a through line from east to west." On Saturday, December 10, the Union army stationed itself on the outskirts of Savannah. Sherman's men had traveled the 250 miles from Atlanta in twenty-six days and had inflicted more than $1 billion worth of damages on Georgia and Georgians. When he entered the city of Savannah some days later, the triumphant Sherman telegraphed President Lincoln to notify him that he was giving him Savannah "as a Christmas present."

1865

The Most Wanted Man in America

Jefferson Davis, former president of the Confederate States of America, might not have been so complacent had he known that the United States government had just placed a $100,000 reward on his head. Not only was he being tracked as the fugitive head of the Confederacy, but he was also wanted as an accomplice to John Wilkes Booth in the assassination of President Abraham Lincoln.

Davis knew that he was being closely pursued, but as far as he or the cabinet members and military personnel traveling with him knew, the enemy army was days behind him. His wife, Varina, recognized the extreme danger that her husband was in, and she was concerned that the large entourage of men and supplies that accompanied their party would slow them down so much that they would eventually be overcome by advance elements of the Union army. More than once Varina warned her husband, "Cut loose from your escort. Go swiftly and alone."

Encamped for the night in a deep forest, Davis carefully considered his situation. Tired, bent over, and looking well beyond his fifty-six years, he was decked out in a clean, gray uniform that matched his graying hair and beard. Stirring the hot coals in the small but brightly burning campfire at his feet, Davis asked one of his traveling companions just exactly where they were. He was advised that the small village of Irwinville, Georgia, was just down the muddy road.

The Davis family had been on the run for more than five weeks now. They had hastily departed from Richmond, Virginia, when intelligence reports revealed that a Union army was marching on the Confederate capital. First by train, then by army wagon and ambulance, Davis, Varina, and a few cabinet members had already passed through Danville, Virginia; Greensboro and Charlotte, North Carolina; backcountry South Carolina; and across the Savannah River into eastern Georgia. Now as they progressed southward toward the Florida border, the foremost thought on Davis's mind was reaching the Gulf of Mexico and eventually Mexico itself. There, with any luck, he could carry on the Confederate cause *in absentia*.

With the dinner meal completed, Davis and Varina prepared to retire for the evening. The men had pitched a makeshift tent for the couple, while they intended to sleep on the ground. Davis removed only his boots and his coat, laid down beside Varina, and instantly dropped off to sleep.

Just before daybreak on May 10, Davis and Varina were awakened by commotion in their camp, followed by distant gunfire, then by the sound of rapidly approaching horses.

Near the perimeter of camp, a sentry belatedly warned that Yankee cavalrymen were in their midst. Mass confusion descended on camp, while Davis pulled on his boots and stepped outside his tent to assess the situation. In the meantime, Varina begged him to mount up and leave the area immediately lest he run the risk of being taken prisoner. Someone told Davis that there was a swamp immediately behind the camp that might provide an escape. Davis vacillated. He did not want to leave his wife and staff, yet he knew what his future held if, indeed, he was captured.

What happened next is one of the great unsolved mysteries of the Civil War. Did Jefferson Davis disguise himself as a woman in order to escape? According to the later testimony of Davis and Varina, Davis was grappling in the darkness of the tent looking for his overcoat when he picked up Varina's shawl instead. Throwing it around his shoulders, he started off rapidly for the swamp. In the meantime, Varina sent a servant woman to carry a bucket behind him to give the illusion that the two figures were fetching water from the swamp.

Suddenly a corporal of the Fourth Michigan Cavalry burst through the flap of Varina's tent looking for Davis. Varina immediately started chatting wildly in an attempt to buy her husband more time to escape. By now, the sun was peeping over the eastern horizon and as he looked outside toward the swamp, the corporal spotted Davis's spurs gleaming in the morning light. He ordered Davis to stop. When he approached the refugee and saw his face, he immediately knew that he had captured the most wanted man in America. Davis was escorted back to his tent where he sadly exclaimed, "God's will be done."

Federal authorities had a different story to tell. James H. Wilson, the general in charge of the cavalry unit that captured Davis, suggested two years after the event that since "the friends of Davis have strenuously denied that he was disguised as a woman, it may not be improper to specify the exact articles of woman's apparel which he had upon him when first seen." Continuing, Wilson wrote that officers present at the time of his capture testified that, "Davis, in addition to his full suit of Confederate gray, had on 'a lady's waterproof cloak, gathered at the waist, with a shawl drawn over the head.'" Wilson concluded, "From these circumstances there seems to be no doubt whatever that Davis sought to avoid capture by assuming the dress of a woman."

> The capital of Georgia is Atlanta, which is also the largest city in the state, with an estimated 2018 population of 491,626 within the city limits.

Whether Davis purposely disguised himself as a woman, or whether, in the confusion to escape, he merely picked up a piece of his wife's clothing will never be known. What history does relate is that, after his capture, Davis, Varina, and the rest of his staff and traveling party were taken first to Macon, then to Savannah, and finally to the federal prison at Fort Monroe, Virginia. Davis had to endure jeers, insults, and profanities from his Union escort. "We'll hang Jeff Davis from a sour apple tree" were the words to one of the ditties that Davis's captors sang in his presence.

Jefferson Davis was incarcerated at Fort Monroe for nearly two years, sometimes in leg irons. The charge that he conspired with John Wilkes Booth to assassinate President Lincoln was eventually dropped, but he still faced the more serious charge of treason. During the months that Jefferson was in prison, Varina worked to obtain clemency for her husband. Finally, in May 1867, all charges against Jefferson Davis were dropped, and he was released from prison. After the tired former president of the Confederacy left the courtroom for a final time, he made plans to travel to New York and eventually to Canada where his children were living with their grandmother.

After the Civil War ended, Davis and Varina returned to the South from Canada, and retired to Biloxi, Mississippi, where Davis wrote *The Rise and Fall of the Confederate Government*. He died at his home, Beauvoir, in 1889 and was survived by Varina, who later moved to New York, donated Beauvoir as a Confederate veterans' home, and pursued a writing career. She died in 1905.

JOHN HERNDON (JOHNNY) MERCER

(1909–1976)

Few American lyricists can boast authorship of such an impressive list of successful hit songs, for both the recording industry and movies, as Savannah's Johnny Mercer. Beginning at age twenty, and for almost a half-century, Mercer wrote lyrics for an estimated one thousand songs, earning him and his co-writers four Academy Awards: "Moon River" (1962) with Henry Mancini; "Days of Wine and Roses" (1963) with Mancini; "In the Cool, Cool, Cool of the Evening" (1952) with Hoagy Carmichael; and "On the Atchison, Topeka, and the Santa Fe" (1947) with Harry Warren. Mercer was undoubtedly one of America's most versatile and prolific songwriters, who wrote or co-wrote such diverse hits as "You Must Have Been a Beautiful Baby," "I'm an Old Cowhand from the Rio Grande," "Fools Rush In," and "Blues in the Night."

Mercer was born into an affluent Savannah family whose roots extended back to colonial days. He was a direct descendant of General Hugh Mercer, a protégé and confidant of George Washington in both the French and Indian War and the Revolution. Although young Johnny attended prestigious private schools in Georgia and Virginia, he was financially unable to attend college due to a reversal in his family's fortune. Instead, he moved to New York, became enamored with "show business," and, after winning a singing contest orchestrated by noted bandleader Paul Whiteman, wrote lyrics for such luminaries as Duke Ellington, Billie Holiday, and Lionel Hampton.

Mercer became a fixture of the "Tin Pan Alley" scene in New York City, and soon found himself chumming around with the likes of Hoagy Carmichael and other rapidly rising musicians and songwriters. For Mercer, the next stop was Hollywood, where he and others founded Capitol Records in 1942 and began working with Bing Crosby, Nat King Cole, and Peggy Lee, among others.

Mercer died following surgery for brain cancer and is buried in Savannah's Bonaventure Cemetery. Savannah's municipal theater is named after Mercer.

1867

A Walk across Georgia

Daylight had just dawned when John Muir rose from his makeshift bed—a "mattress of Long Moss" covered with a roof made from rushes—that he had hastily built in the middle of Bonaventure Cemetery in Savannah, Georgia. In the deathly silence of the graveyard, as he sleepily watched the sun peek above the eastern horizon, Muir's ears were only attuned to his growling stomach, and he figured he was just about as near to starvation as he had ever been in his twenty-nine years on earth.

Earlier, upon crossing into Georgia from Tennessee, Muir had written:

Am now fairly out of the mountains ... The Chattahoochee River is richly embanked with massive, bossy, dark green oaks, and wreathed with a dense growth of muscadine grapevines, whose ornate foliage, so well adapted to bank embroidery was enriched with other interweaving species of vines and brightly colored flowers.

Keeping a journal as he traveled, Muir, who years later would attain worldwide recognition as the founder of the Sierra Club, continued his walk from the Tennessee border through Georgia, and when he arrived in Savannah he had only one dollar in his pocket. After spending his first night in "the meanest looking lodging-house that I could find on account of its cheapness," he realized that his money would be better used for food than for lodging, and that even by spending them sparingly, his funds would almost certainly not last until he received more from home. Now, almost a week later, his dollar was gone, and he had eaten nothing but crackers for the past several meals. His normally gaunt body looked a few pounds leaner than it did a month earlier when he had departed Indianapolis on what he described as "a joyful and free . . . thousand-mile walk to the Gulf of Mexico."

On his second day in Savannah, Muir had hiked the 4 miles of country road to the cemetery and set up camp within its walls to await the money that was to be forthcoming from his brother back home in Wisconsin. Every day he walked back to the post office in Savannah to check on his mail, and every day he returned, disappointed, to the cemetery to prepare for another foodless night among the dead.

Actually, Muir, an aspiring botanist who had received his education at the University of Wisconsin, really liked the old cemetery. In the book *A Thousand-Mile Walk to the Gulf*, based on the journal he kept during his long hike, he called it "so beautiful that almost any sensible person would choose to dwell here with the dead rather than with the lazy, disorderly living." Moreover, he wrote:

> The most conspicuous glory of Bonaventure is its noble avenue of live-oaks. They are the most magnificent planted trees I have ever seen, about fifty feet high and perhaps three or four feet in diameter, with broad spreading leafy heads. . . . There are also thousands of smaller trees and clustered bushes, covered almost from sight in the glorious brightness of their own light. The place is half surrounded by the salt marshes and islands of the river, their reeds and sedges making a delightful fringe. Many bald eagles roost among the trees along the side of the marsh. Their screams are heard every morning, joined with the noise of crows and the songs of countless warblers, hidden deep in their dwellings of leafy bowers. Large flocks of butterflies, all kinds of happy insects, seem to be in a perfect fever of joy and sportive gladness. The whole place seems like a center of life. The dead do not reign there alone.

One day, after spending nearly a week in the cemetery, Muir entered the post office in Savannah to discover that his money had finally arrived; he was ecstatic. "Gladly I pocketed my money," he wrote, "and had not gone along the street more than a few rods before I met a very large negro woman with a tray of gingerbread, in which I immediately invested some of my new wealth, and walked rejoicingly, munching along the street, making no attempt to conceal the pleasure I had in eating."

John Muir's 1867 journey across Georgia took him from Blairsville in the north, through Gainesville, Athens, and

Thomson, to Augusta. From there he followed the Savannah River to Savannah and his cemetery adventures. Eventually he took a steamship to Florida. Muir was impressed by Georgians, and he wrote, "Of the people of the States

that I have now passed, I best like the Georgians. They have charming manners, and their dwellings are mostly larger and better than those of adjacent States." He was equally impressed by the vast array of wild animals and unfamiliar plant life that he observed throughout the state, writing in his journal that "scarce a familiar face appears among all the flowers of the day's walk."

While in Florida, Muir became ill, probably from malaria. He later sailed to Cuba then crossed the Isthmus of Panama and sailed up America's West Coast to San Francisco. California became his home, and it was there that he did the majority of his conservation work. He was influential in the creation of Yosemite, Sequoia, and Mount Rainier National Parks, and developed a controversial theory on the glaciation of the Yosemite Valley. He founded the Sierra Club in 1892 to do "something for wilderness and make the mountains glad."

John Muir dedicated his entire adult life to conservation and wilderness preservation—a crusade that began when he took a thousand-mile walk across southeastern America and was awed by the unique beauty, the places, and the people of Georgia.

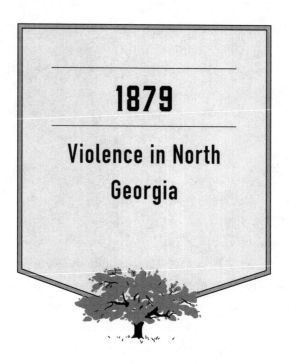

1879

Violence in North Georgia

Twenty-six-year-old Joseph Standing, a missionary in the Mormon Church, awoke from a troubled sleep and quickly recounted in his mind the recurrent dream that had robbed him of rest for the past few weeks. It was a strange dream—almost a nightmare—and while he could never recall its exact details, he felt that it was a premonition of things to come. Attempting to explain the dream to a friend, Standing told him that "clouds of intense blackness gathered overhead and around me," and that he always awoke from the encounters "without my being shown the end of trouble." When some of Standing's local Mormon converts began to shun him on account of "a sense of great fearfulness," the young evangelist grew more concerned that his future in Georgia would be precarious.

Standing realized that his life was in danger. Stationed in the rolling mountains of North Georgia among predominantly Scots-Irish Protestants, he and other missionaries who preceded him shared a common knowledge that Mormons were not welcome in the region, or, for that matter, anywhere else east of Utah. The church's acceptance and promulgation of polygamy was the primary objection that other Christian sects had with Mormon beliefs. And for years Mormons had paid the supreme price for spreading their doctrine. Thirty-five years earlier, the church's founder, Joseph Smith, had been murdered in Illinois by a band of irate citizens, and during the early months of 1879, Mormon establishments in Kentucky and North Carolina witnessed serious attacks. It seemed to most Mormon missionaries in the field that the potential for violence simply went with the job of converting people of other faiths to Mormonism.

> *Georgia lies entirely within the Eastern Time Zone.*

Joseph Standing had recently been given an assistant to help him in his missionary work. Rudger Clawson, the twenty-two-year-old son of a prominent Mormon churchman, had recently arrived in Varnell Station, the small village where Standing operated his ministry in Georgia. In addition to Whitfield County, the pair of ministers traveled the mountains and valleys of the surrounding region of North Georgia in search of converts.

On Sunday, July 20, 1879, Standing and Clawson were on their way to a church meeting at Rome, Georgia, situated about 40 miles south of Varnell. They were walking down a trail bounded on each side by thick forest, and they were busily engaged in conversation about the upcoming meeting when twelve heavily armed men burst out of the woods. Members of this mob quickly surrounded the two young missionaries and commanded them to retrace their steps toward Varnell. Several miles back up the trail, the leader of the mob, James Faucett, ordered the group to rest and took the opportunity to warn Standing and Clawson that, "if we ever find you in this part of the country we will hang you by the neck like dogs."

Apparently, the vigilantes originally intended to take Standing and Clawson back to Varnell, place them on the next train out of town, and send them on their way instilled with enough fear never to come back. But when the group prepared to continue their journey, Standing somehow commandeered a pistol from a guard and demanded that all of the men surrender to him. Before the words got out of his mouth, one of his captors fired a single, but fatal, shot to Standing's head. The young Mormon died instantly. Members of the mob gathered around the body as one of them laughingly exclaimed, "This is terrible; that he should have killed himself in such a manner."

For a few tense moments, Clawson's life hung in the balance. Some of the mob wanted to kill him too, but finally, they decided to release him so that he could forewarn prospective missionaries who might take Standing's place that the same fate awaited them. Clawson cut through the forest, with the scathing remarks of one of the gang members ringing in his ears: "The government of the United States is against you, and there is no law in Georgia for Mormons." In time, he came upon a friend's house where he borrowed a horse. The terrified missionary rode off to the nearest telegraph station and wired the tragic news to his superiors in Salt Lake City.

When local law enforcement authorities received word of the murder, they dispatched a coroner's jury to the site of the crime. The coroner's report was terse and to the point, declaring that "the deceased came to his death by gun and pistol shots ... inflicted upon the head and neck ... and wounds consisting of twenty shots or more." When Clawson heard the report, he surmised that following his own release from the mob, the rest of the vigilantes fired shots into Standing's dead body so that no single one of them could be charged with the crime.

Clawson took Standing's remains back to Salt Lake City where funeral services were held in the giant Mormon Temple and were attended by several thousand mourners. Standing was buried in the old city cemetery. While the young martyr was being eulogized by his friends and church superiors in Utah, the suspects in the murder case were being rounded up for trial in Whitfield County.

For weeks after it occurred, Standing's murder was all that people in Georgia talked about, and all the state's newspapers reported on the incident. The *Atlanta Constitution* editorialized the crime as "a cold and premeditated one, no cause having been given other than that the Mormons had made some converts and created some disturbances in families in the neighborhood." Moreover, the newspaper called the crime "absolutely and utterly without excuse, and [it] should be condemned and punished." Taking the opposite view was the *Catoosa Courier*, a small-town paper that reported "Mr. Standing's preaching and teaching have been of such immoral character that the good citizens ... could not stand any longer the bad influence that his preaching had upon the female portion of the neighborhood."

Finally, by mid-October, the three apparent ringleaders of the mob that captured and killed Standing had been arrested and were being held in the Whitfield County jail for trial. More than 150 citizens were called for jury duty before a jury could be seated. Rudger Clawson returned to Georgia for the trial and was the star witness for the prosecution. But despite the preponderance of evidence that Joseph Standing was murdered and his body mutilated by some or all of the defendants, one of the men was found not guilty, and all murder charges against the others were dropped. A high-ranking Mormon official said the proceedings were "a farce of a trial." He added that the "witnesses as a general thing testified inconsistently or biased their testimony for the defense, after a lengthy investigations [sic], which was bitterly in opposition to the truth a verdict of not guilty was rendered and prisoners discharged."

Amid threats upon his own life, Clawson left town immediately and returned to Utah. More than one hundred of his Georgia Mormon converts followed him, but others stayed behind to continue the fight for what they thought was right. Clawson went on to serve time in prison when he was convicted on polygamy charges, a verdict that was upheld by the United States Supreme Court. After his release he attained the high-ranking position of Apostle within the Mormon Church, holding the appointment until he died in 1943.

Today a monument placed on the supposed murder site of Joseph Standing memorializes this sad chapter in Georgia history.

1882

An Interview with
Oscar Wilde

On July 4, 1882, in the midst of one of the worst heat waves ever to visit Georgia, an obviously agitated Oscar Wilde sat in his hotel room trying to keep calm during an interview with a reporter from the *Atlanta Constitution*. Wilde had been traveling the Deep South for almost a month now, and although he personally had nothing against the region nor its inhabitants, the lack of attendance at his lectures, the tremendous heat, and his busy travel schedule had just about worn him out.

Twenty-eight years old, Wilde was an Irish playwright, novelist, and poet. He is best remembered today for his well-received book *The Picture of Dorian Gray*. Wilde had arrived in the United States in January 1882 with plans to tour America during the next year and to give lectures on "aestheticism," defined by the dictionary as "the pursuit of the sensuously beautiful." By July his southern tour had carried him to less-than-packed houses in Vicksburg, New Orleans, Galveston, Houston, Mobile, Birmingham, Columbus, Macon, and now, Atlanta. In an attempt to explain the reason for such a small turnout

in Macon, a local newspaper reporter there had complained that Wilde lacked "that important essential to all lecturers, humor" and suggested that this oversight "put an air brake to anything like applause" from the bored audiences.

Wilde hoped that his talks would be better received in Atlanta, particularly if he first gave an extensive interview to the city's largest newspaper. The reporter wrote that the tall long-haired Wilde was dressed in a "black velvet jacket . . . white waist coat with gray woolen pantaloons . . . a monster moonlight green tie . . . socks [of] exquisite silk and his shoes [like] dainty gaiters." Wilde sat in an oversized rocking chair on the far side of the room. For nearly an hour Wilde and the journalist engaged in conversation, covering everything from the proper manner in which to celebrate the Fourth of July, to Wilde's opinions of Jefferson Davis, to the poet's conviction that the majority of Americans lacked a proper knowledge of art.

The journalist reported the poet's thoughts in the July 4 edition of the newspaper:

> I don't think that anything so fine as the Declaration of Independence should be celebrated at all if it cannot be celebrated in a very noble manner. Amongst

the most artistic things that any city can do is to celebrate by pageant any great eras in its history. Why should not the 4th of July pageant in Atlanta be as fine as the Mardi Gras in New Orleans? Indeed, a pageant is the most perfect school of art for a people.... I am afraid that the only pageants that most American cities have a hope of seeing are the glaring processions of their traveling circuses, and I feel they deserve something very much better.

To the reporter's surprise, Wilde had an impressive knowledge of the American Civil War. When the conversation proceeded to the subject of Jefferson Davis, late president of the Confederate States of America, the Irishman remarked that he had a great admiration for Davis and that the ideals of the Confederacy reminded him of his own people's struggles for independence from Great Britain. Quoting Wilde, the reporter wrote:

He [Jefferson Davis] impressed me very much as a man of keenest intellect, and a man fairly to be a leader of men on account of a personality that is as simple as it is strong, and an enthusiasm that is as fervent as it is faultless. We in Ireland are fighting for the principle of autonomy against empire, for independence against centralization, for the principle for which the South fought.... The principles for which Mr. Davis and the South went to war cannot suffer defeat.

Shortly after the interview, Wilde proceeded to DeGive's Opera House and spoke to a large audience. Dressed in "a suit of rich, black velvet, knee britches, silk hose, lace waistbands, patent leather slippers with silver buckles, and an immense watch fob," the effeminate poet admonished his listeners:

> . . . [to make] the common articles of everyday life beautiful. If we neglect the useful and common things of life and wait for art to be bestowed upon the more expensive things, art will always be rich. . . . It is wrong to suppose that there is opposition between the useful and the beautiful. . . . Begin by making simple things beautiful and a true art will be built up. A city should have a museum . . . where everything is beautiful and where one could have all the best work of artisans before him. . . . All workmen should go there, and their work will be done with more pleasure, and it will be better done.

From Atlanta, Wilde and his entourage traveled to Savannah where he spoke to another sizable crowd of Georgians who were mixed in their acceptance of a man who wore ruffles on his shirt, velvet knee britches, and had unkempt hair that reached down to his shoulders. At the next stop, in Augusta, the Irishman spoke at the Opera House, once again dressed in his eccentric attire. In writing of the performance, a reporter for the local newspaper lamented, "To the mind of the audience, his style was horrible."

Georgia's motto is "Wisdom, Justice, and Moderation."

After his Augusta speech, Wilde left Georgia. It is not clear how much money he made from his American tour, which consisted of about two hundred engagements, including those in Georgia. It is possible that he made as much as $30,000, a princely sum considering that the annual salary for the president of the United States was only $50,000. People probably paid to see him more out of curiosity than anything else since his message was never widely accepted.

In November 1900, eighteen years after he returned to Europe from the United States, Oscar Wilde died penniless in France at the age of forty-six. His last words supposedly were, "It really would be more than the English could stand if another century began and I were still alive. I am dying as I lived—beyond my means."

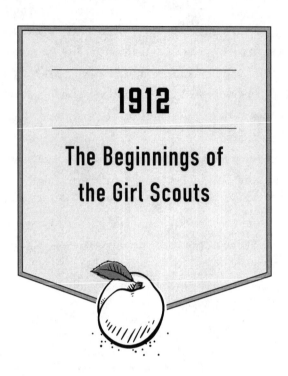

1912

The Beginnings of the Girl Scouts

Juliette "Daisy" Gordon Low was a woman in a hurry. Ever since her departure from Europe several weeks earlier, only one goal occupied her mind. Now, as the petite, fifty-one-year-old widow approached her towering three-story home located on the corner of Bull Street and Oglethorpe Avenue in downtown Savannah, she was poised to act on that mission and make it a reality.

Daisy barely had time to greet her family and servants before she rushed to the telephone and placed a call to her cousin, Nina Pape. Blurting into the phone, the excited woman declared, "Come right over! I've got something for the girls of Savannah, and all America, and all the world, and we're going to start it tonight!" Three days later, on March 12, 1912, in the presence of eighteen young girls sitting in the parlor of the big house on Bull Street, Daisy Low organized what later became the Girl Scouts. Juliette Gordon Low's niece, Daisy Gordon, was installed as the first girl scout in the United States.

Low's journey from her Savannah childhood as daughter of one of the most affluent families in the city to her intense determination to form an organization that would benefit girls of all ages, races, and social standings, was a long and sometimes tortuous one. Born in Savannah on Halloween day, 1860, Juliette, called Daisy when she was growing up, barely remembered the agony of the Civil War as Northern armies rolled roughshod thorough Georgia. Fortunately, when General William T. Sherman's destructive march from Atlanta to Savannah wreaked financial and personal ruin upon hundreds of Georgia families, the Gordons had survived and lived to see brighter and more bountiful days.

Tragedy struck Daisy when she was twenty-five years old. For some while, a series of ear infections had caused her prolonged and excruciating pain. At the time several American physicians—mostly in the North—were experimenting with silver nitrate as a potential cure for ear abscesses. Daisy talked her uninformed doctor into applying the chemical to her ear, and the dangerous and unsuccessful treatment left her deaf on that side. Daisy's partial deafness only served to reinforce her love for life. As if nothing had happened, she continued her busy schedule of attending practically every Savannah social event, and at one of these gala functions, she met her future husband.

William McKay Low, who maintained a residence and business office in Savannah, was the son of a wealthy British shipping family. After a brief courtship, Daisy and William, over the protests of her parents, announced their engagement. On December 21, 1886, the couple was married at Savannah's historic Christ Episcopal Church. And then once again, tragedy visited Daisy. When the happy newlyweds exited the church, amid a barrage of rice being tossed by well-wishers, a single grain entered Daisy's good ear and embedded itself deep within the hearing canal. Efforts to extract the rice failed, and within a few short months, Daisy's hearing in that ear was gone as well.

Deafness aside, Daisy's next few years were among the happiest in her life. She and William Low maintained three separate residences in England and traveled Europe extensively during the early days of their marriage. After a dozen or so years of marriage, however, the union between Daisy and William began to fall apart. With increasing frequency, William took off alone on hunting expeditions, while Daisy, still very much a social butterfly, continued to entertain her friends and participate in charitable work. In 1898, after returning to England from a trip to Florida where she assisted her mother with the establishment of a hospital for Spanish-American War veterans, Daisy was devastated to learn that William had taken a mistress and requested a divorce. However, before it could be granted, he died, but not prior to leaving his entire estate—and a quite sizable one at that—to the mistress.

Embarrassed by her failed marriage, as well as the humiliation of helplessly watching her husband's legacy go to another woman, Daisy elected to maintain her residence in Great Britain rather than returning to family and friends in Savannah. For the next several years, she lived alone yet still pursuing a social life. She was visited by nieces and nephews from the United States and embarked on new artistic adventures, including sculpting and metalworking. Then in

May 1911, she made the acquaintance of General Sir Robert Baden-Powell, a man who would change her life forever.

Baden-Powell had established the Boy Scouts movement in England in 1908. Two years later with the assistance of his sister, Agnes, he founded the Girl Guides—an organization similar to the Boy Scouts. Daisy was fascinated with the new program and visited Sir Robert and Agnes often, learning all she could about the newly formed girls' movement. She was totally captivated by the man and his vision for young women. One month after her initial meeting with Baden-Powell, she wrote:

> Today, in the few moments I have had to myself, my mind has dwelt irresistibly on B-P. A sort of intuition comes over me that he believes I might make more out of my life and that he has ideas which, if I follow them, will open a more useful sphere of work before me in the future. . . . I told him a little about my futile efforts to be of use and the shame I feel when I think of how much I could do, yet how little I accomplish. . . . He looked so kindly when he said, "There are little stars that guide us on, although we do not realize it."

When Daisy returned to her Savannah home in 1912 and organized the Girl Guides in America, she carried with her the *British Girl Guide Handbook* written by Sir Robert and Agnes. She later hired W. J. Hoxie to rewrite the manual and re-title it *How Girls Can Help Their Country*. The Girl Guides saw significant growth throughout 1912. Troops began to form all along America's Eastern Seaboard, and in May 1912, the Girl Guides in America made their first public appearance in Savannah wearing their official uniform—a dark blue duck with light blue ties.

In 1913 the Girl Guides in America changed their name to the Girl Scouts, and National Headquarters were established in Washington, DC. By 1915 the organization claimed more than five thousand members, and Daisy had officially become its president at the first annual convention held in DC. She also became the representative for America when the International Council of Girl Guides was formed in 1919.

For several years Daisy personally financed the entire Girl Scout movement. As the enterprise continued to rapidly grow, however, the executive board decided that a powerful fund-raiser was needed to increase income for expenses. Although cookies had been locally sold on a limited basis for several years, the first nationally franchised cookie sale was held in the late 1930s. Today, hundreds of millions of boxes are sold annually.

Juliette "Daisy" Gordon Low died on January 17, 1927, but her legacy lives on. In 1948 the US Postal Service issued a three-cent stamp in her honor. More than 750,000 of these stamps were sold in Savannah on the first day of issue. A bust of Juliette Gordon Low was placed in Georgia's Hall of Fame in 1974, and she was inducted into the National Women's Hall of Fame in 1979. In 1983 the Juliette Gordon Low Federal Complex was opened in Savannah. This was only the second federal building ever to be named after a woman. In 2012, President Barack Obama posthumously awarded the Presidential Medal of Freedom, the highest civilian award in the nation, to this phenomenal woman who was years ahead of her time in visualizing the true importance and potential of females in the American dream.

Entering its second century of service, the Girl Scouts proudly claims a membership of around 2.6 million girls. It is estimated that in excess of 50 million American women, past and present, have been affiliated with this organization.

1914

The Legacy of
Stone Mountain

Helen Plane, the socially prominent president of the Atlanta chapter of the United Daughters of the Confederacy, was extremely excited as she placed the June 14, 1914, issue of the *Atlanta Georgian* on her kitchen table and quickly turned to the editorial page. She had been told that this issue of the paper would be carrying an article of great interest to her. Unbeknownst to Plane, in just two short weeks, the world would be thrown into vicious far-ranging warfare when the archduke of Austria was assassinated in far-away Sarajevo. But today, the Atlanta matron's mind was on her beloved Stone Mountain project. She was excited that Georgia soon would have such a grand Confederate monument.

Plane scanned the editorial page and quickly found the article of importance. Written by John Temple Graves, the prestigious editor of the *New York American*, the piece had been picked up for reprint by southern papers everywhere because of the intense interest among southerners in its subject matter. Plane adjusted her glasses and read with pleasure:

To the veterans of the dead Confederacy, to the daughters and sons, and to all who revere the memories of that historic and immortal struggle, I bring today the suggestion of a great memorial, perfectly simple, perfectly feasible, and which if realized will give to the Confederate soldier and his memories the most majestic monument, set in the most magnificent frame in all the world. . . . Stone Mountain is distinctly one of the wonders of the world. . . . It is a mountain of solid granite one mile from its summit to its base. Much of Atlanta has been builded from it, and there is enough left to build ten more Atlantas without touching the lofty spot that is nearest to the sun. On the steep side of Stone Mountain, facing northward, there is a sheer declivity that rises or falls from 900 to 1,000 feet. Here, then, is Nature's matchless plan for a memorial. On this steep side let those who love the Southern dead combine to have the engineers cut a projection 30 feet wide and 100 feet deep. Into this projection and as high as it may be made, let us . . . chisel an heroic statue, 70 feet high, of the Confederate soldier in the nearest resemblance to Robert E. Lee. . . . And there—1,200 feet above the plain, let us place the old gray granite hat upon that noble head with its grand eyes turned toward Atlanta . . . and from this godlike eminence let our Confederate hero calmly look history and the future in the face. . . . There will be no monument in all the world like this, our monument to the Confederate dead. None so majestic, none so magnificently framed, and none that will more powerfully attract the interest and admiration of those who have a soul.

Plane took the reading glasses from her nose and dried her moist eyes with a handkerchief. Here, at last, was an eloquent plea for the completion of the project that she had advocated for the past five years. With the likes of John Temple Graves behind it, perhaps now the job would start.

Plane, encouraged by the positive reception that Graves's article received around the country, soon met with renowned sculptor Gutzon Borglum. She asked his advice on the feasibility of the project, and was disappointed when Borglum replied that he thought the proposal was ridiculous and that a sculpture of General Lee's head on those thousands of square feet of granite would look like "a postage stamp on a barn." Borglum then suggested instead that Stone Mountain be carved to reflect hundreds of Confederate soldiers marching across its vertical face.

In 1916, soon after meeting with Borglum, members of the United Daughters of the Confederacy negotiated a lease of the Stone Mountain property from its owners, the Venable family. Part of the agreement called for the sculpture to be completed by 1928. Although World War I and its economic aftermath delayed an immediate start on the monument, a private organization was formed to oversee the project, Borglum was officially hired, and a massive fund-raising effort was launched. Borglum began work on the carving in 1923. The following year President Calvin Coolidge signed the Stone Mountain Memorial Coinage Act into law, whereby backers of the project could raise a potential $2.5 million from the sale of five million commemorative half-dollars.

By 1925 the honeymoon phase between the Stone Mountain Memorial Association and Gutzon Borglum had ended. Although Robert E. Lee's face had been completed and dedicated on January 19, 1924, the anniversary of the general's birth, difficulties between Borglum and the association caused the sculptor to resign and move on to his Mount Rushmore project in South Dakota, bringing him eventual fame.

> Georgia's state nickname is "The Empire State of the South."

On April 1, 1925, a new sculptor, Augustus Lukeman, was hired by the Stone Mountain Memorial Association and began work on Stone Mountain. Realizing the magnitude of the assignment—hundreds of individual soldiers marching across the face of the cliff as proposed by Borglum—Lukeman suggested that a simple motif of three recognized Confederate leaders grace the mountain: Robert E. Lee, Thomas "Stonewall" Jackson, and Jefferson Davis. The association approved his design, and Lukeman went to work.

As the year 1928 rapidly approached, it was clear that the entire sculpture could not be completed within the constraints placed upon the project by the lease agreement with the Venables. With only the faces of Davis, Lee, and Lee's horse, Traveler, completed by the imposed date, Lukeman pressed for an extension on the project. They could not reach an agreement, however, and the property reverted to the Venable family. It remained under their ownership until

1958, when the State of Georgia bought Stone Mountain and surrounding property for $1,125,000 and formed a government authority to oversee the sculpture's completion.

In 1963, selecting from among nine different new designs, the state hired Walker Kirtland Hancock to fill the vacancy of chief sculptor. By then new technology was available, and within seven years, the massive carving on the face of Stone Mountain was virtually completed. In the meantime, the state acquired more land around the base of the mountain and designed and imple-mented many additional attractions including a museum, a fully functional steamboat, campsites, a large motel, and convention facilities. The carving was finally completed in 1969. As planned, it depicts "Stonewall" Jackson, Jefferson Davis, and Robert E. Lee on horseback.

Today, millions of tourists visit Stone Mountain Park and its attractions every year.

DEAN RUSK

(1909–1994)

Dean Rusk served in the position of US secretary of state longer than anyone else in American history except Cordell Hull. Born in Cherokee County, Rusk graduated from Davidson College in North Carolina in 1931. As a Rhodes Scholar at Oxford, he earned both bachelor of science and master of arts degrees. While attending Oxford, war clouds were brewing across Europe, and as Rusk observed many of his fellow students endorsing a stringent policy of appeasement toward Hitler's increasingly hostile rhetoric and threats, his mind was being challenged and conditioned for his future job as secretary of state during the Vietnam War. One of his biographers, Loch K. Johnson, summarized Rusk's eye-opening observations at Oxford, and the actual commencement of World War II which soon followed, writing "The experience had a profound effect on Rusk's worldview and would make him a determined opponent of efforts to meet acts of aggression with offers of appeasement."

After Oxford, Rusk taught international relations and served as dean of faculty at Mills College in California, at the same time studying law at the University of California, Berkeley. He joined the army even before Pearl Harbor was attacked and was assigned to the 3rd Infantry Division. He soon transferred to Military Intelligence in the Asian Theater, and at the war's end he transferred once again, this time to the War Department in Washington, DC, with an opportunity to assist General George Marshall.

After Rusk presided over the Rockefeller Foundation for several years, John F. Kennedy selected him as secretary of state, a role Rusk kept through the end of Lyndon Johnson's administration. The Vietnam War dominated much of Rusk's attention as secretary, and, remembering his days at Oxford, he continued to maintain his posture of non-appeasement, becoming one of the nation's most outspoken advocates of American involvement in the conflict, a position that was criticized by many. After his Washington, DC, tenure, Rusk retired to Athens, where he taught international law at the University of Georgia.

1933

Bedspread Alley

During the Depression, salesmen and travelers venturing down Highway 41 between Dalton and Cartersville could see colorful chenille bedspreads hanging on clotheslines, drying in the sunshine. Known as "Bedspread Alley," this track was an enjoyable way to find a bedspread to buy. The Whitfield County mountain women who started selling their bedspreads to make ends meet never dreamed their Depression-era tufting trade would eventually turn into today's multibillion-dollar textile industry.

In the early twentieth century, Northwest Georgia consisted of rolling hills, poor farmland, hard-packed clay soil, and struggling cotton and steel mills. By streamlining the struggling cotton mills, the bedspread industry turned native raw materials into finished products without a big investment in machinery. Income from bedspreads became instrumental to the survival of families during the Great Depression.

The origins of Georgia's bedspread industry can be traced back to Catherine Evans Whitener, who first decided to sell her popular handmade bedspreads for $2.50 each. By 1930 demand had become so great that entire families were hired to hand tuft Catherine's spreads for ten to twenty-five cents per spread. Work began before breakfast, continued through all hours of the day, and at night until Grandma, Grandpa, aunt, cousin, and little sister were too tired to continue. Seeing the profits Catherine was bringing in, other women began making and selling spreads of their own. Soon these local entrepreneurs were producing so many spreads that they had to hire haulers to take the spreads and sell them to merchants.

The cottage bedspread industry grew rapidly. Each year the demand increased and more women began to make spreads. Spreads from Whitfield County were sold in all the exclusive eastern shops. Mrs. J. T. Bates stated she simply shipped fifteen spreads to John Wanamaker's department store in New York. On a plain piece of tablet paper, she made out a bill for $98.15 and put it in with the spreads. Although Bates had made no previous contact whatsoever with the store, Wanamaker sent her a check for $98.15.

The idea of commercializing the manufacture of bedspreads came from successful businesswoman Mrs. H. L. Jarvis. She established Dalton's first bedspread manufacturing "headquarters" where women could bring their spreads for sale and distribution. Jarvis soon gave Wanamaker's store the exclusive privilege of selling these spreads in New York, which proved to be a successful marketing tool. Receipts for bedspreads shipped from Whitfield County in 1923–1924 exceeded the total value of the county's cotton crop.

By 1933 there were approximately thirty manufacturers of bedspreads for trade and interstate commerce in the United States. At least twenty-five were located in or around Dalton, Georgia, and at least 95 percent of all candlewick spreads manufactured in the United States were manufactured in the Dalton proximity. The manufacturers of candlewick bedspreads maintained no machinery, because the actual manufacture of spreads was done by independent outside workers who used a tufting needle and tufted the yarn into sheets, tracing designs that had been marked on the sheeting. Designs were often replica heirlooms dating back to the colonial time period.

Manufacturers bought sheeting and colored yarns and cut the sheeting into the proper lengths for a bedspread. The sheeting and yarn were then distributed to workers who either came to the plant for it or received it from the haulers who carried out the materials by car loads to local "tufters." By April 1933 the best workers could make up to three bedspreads per day by working eight- to ten-hour days; they earned twenty-four cents per day.

As the bedspread industry grew around Dalton, Singer Sewing Machine Company in nearby Chattanooga took an

interest. Glen Looper modified the single needle commercial Singer so that it would tuft thick yarn into unbleached muslin without tearing the fabric. An attached knife would cut the loop. The company quickly developed machines that used four, then eight, then twenty-four, and then eventually 1,500 needles to make the parallel rows of tufting known as "chenille."

The advent of the Singer tufting machine, combined with the passage of the 1933 minimum wage law, pulled tufters from their homes in the surrounding hillsides into mills in town. As a result, manufacturers could no longer afford to pay hourly wages to single women producing the spreads. Eventually a self-employed tufter working an average of eight hours per day would earn only five cents per four- to six-ounce spread.

Many of the women who did not want to go to work in the town mills took matters into their own hands by converting their own sewing machines into tufting machines, like Catherine Evans Whitener, or by joining the growing tufters' movement. This women's movement began when Mrs. S. H. Mantooth, mother of ten children, contacted R. Noel Steed, solicitor general in Chatsworth, to enlist his help. She lamented that she could now earn no more than $1.25 per week, whereas she used to make $3.50 to $4.00 per week. In the early days of "Bedspread Alley," the pay scale was eight cents per ounce of thread worked into a sixty-weave cloth. Due to the advancement of machinery, thousands of spreads were believed to be made for as little as twelve to fourteen cents each. When the local tufters asked Dalton attorney, R. Carter Pittman for help, he told them, "Your only remedy is in organization: what one woman says doesn't mean a thing. But if what that woman says is backed by 20,000 others, then you can accomplish something."

In August 1936, two thousand candlewick bedspread makers met at the Dalton courthouse to plan a "revolt against the starvation wages"—$1.25 to $1.75 per week—paid them by the manufacturers of the flourishing bedspread industry. A New York man who was passing through the area at the time saw the notice of the meeting in a newspaper and volunteered to donate up to $200 to finance the tufters' organization. Several manufacturers were present at the meeting; some even expressed a willingness to cooperate with workers to raise the pay scale.

When the market for bedspreads gradually declined in the 1950s and 1960s, the carpet industry took its place. When more needles were added to the sewing machines that tufted bedspreads, they could be used to tuft carpet. Today, Northwest Georgia is a leader in the worldwide carpet and tufting industry.

Modern travelers can still venture down "Bedspread Alley" south of Dalton and examine a few multicolored homemade bedspreads for sale right off the clotheslines. Though the bedspread cottage industry has waned, this stretch of Highway 41 serves as a vivid reminder of how a local tufting trade matured into a national textile industry.

1945

The Death of a President

As his private train pulled into the town's tiny station on Good Friday, March 30, 1945, Franklin Delano Roosevelt was glad to be back in the place that he had been visiting periodically for the past twenty years. Roosevelt had first visited Warm Springs, Georgia, in October 1924. On that occasion FDR, at the time a wealthy New York banker, lawyer, and former assistant secretary of the Navy, sought to test the area's medicinal waters, seeking to relieve the paralysis left from the polio he had suffered three years earlier. Back then the spa consisted of a dilapidated forty-six-room hotel, fifteen small cottages, overgrown lawns, and abandoned cottages.

When he returned in 1945, sixty-three-year-old Franklin Delano Roosevelt was a very sick man. Yet, other than his closest friends and associates, few who clamored around the ever-popular president realized the full extent of his illness.

Hundreds of local folks were on hand to greet their thirty-second president at the train station. They watched intently as he slowly descended the train's steps, laboriously climbed into the back seat of a waiting automobile, and was whisked off to the Little White House, located atop Pine Mountain just outside town.

Within minutes after the presidential party reached the Little White House, FDR was in bed, resting up from the exhausting twenty-hour train ride from Washington, DC, to Georgia. That evening, his personal physician, Lieutenant Commander Howard Bruenn, and his private secretary, William Hassett, solemnly discussed their boss's health. "He is slipping away from us and no earthly power can keep him here," exclaimed Hassett. Dr. Bruenn responded that it was his belief that although FDR was in failing health "he could be saved if measures were adopted to rescue him from certain mental strains and emotional influences." But Roosevelt had just been reelected to an unprecedented fourth term as president and the war in Europe and the Far East was still raging. If anything, FDR's stress factors could only get worse.

The next morning, when Hassett delivered the government mail pouch from Washington, he was surprised to find FDR looking almost like his old self. Chatting with his two cousins Margaret Suckley and Laura Delano, Roosevelt seemed prepared to handle the work at hand. By noon, he had digested all of the official news, read every letter, and dictated several responses. When Hassett saw the president again at five o'clock in the evening, however, he found his leader's appearance to be "worn, weary, exhausted." It seemed that after one o'clock or so in the afternoon, the president simply lost all of his energy. The completion of any task, no matter how simple or small, seemed to bring him intense misery.

As Easter Sunday, April 1, 1945, dawned in Warm Springs, President Roosevelt announced that he felt well enough to attend church services in the nearby chapel. However, even with the assistance of his personal valet, Arthur Prettyman, it took FDR more than an hour to get bathed, shaved, and dressed for the service. Wearing a gray suit with a blue tie and seated in his ever-present wheelchair, he arrived at the chapel just before eleven o'clock, accompanied by his two cousins and three Secret Service agents. The rest of the day was pleasant, and when FDR was advised that a southern-style barbecue, complete with an old-fashioned minstrel show, was going to be held on April 12, he enthusiastically replied, "Count me in. I'll go."

The following days were busy ones. President Roosevelt kept in constant communication over war matters with government leaders in Washington, as well as with Great Britain's prime minister, Winston Churchill, and with the marshal of the Soviet Union, Josef Stalin. He held press conferences and was even visited by the president of the Philippines and the US Secretary of the Treasury, Henry Morgenthau. But the visit that he cherished the most was the one from his longtime lady friend, Lucy Mercer Rutherford. Lucy, with whom FDR had maintained a secret affair since the time he served as assistant secretary of the navy, lived in neighboring South Carolina, and she had always made it a point to visit with Roosevelt whenever he traveled to Warm Springs. The affair had almost caused a breakup between Roosevelt and his wife, Eleanor, when she discovered the relationship shortly after it had begun. For the past twenty-seven years, she had assumed that Franklin and Lucy's liaison was over, but a few days later, she was to find out otherwise.

> The state bird is the brown thrasher (Toxostoma rufum).

Lucy had brought an artist with her to Warm Springs who, on April 12—the same day as the barbecue and minstrel show—visited the Little White House to paint a portrait of FDR. Roosevelt's two cousins were in the room visiting, but they paid little attention as Lucy and FDR gazed at each other with the same love in their eyes that had been sparked thirty years earlier. Suddenly Roosevelt declared, "I have a terrific headache." Lucy noticed that he looked strange and exclaimed, "Franklin, are you alright?" Before the words left her mouth, FDR slumped over in his chair, his eyes wide open in the hollow stare of a man who has just had a stroke.

Dr. Bruenn was the first medical professional to arrive at FDR's side. He checked the president's blood pressure and found it was extremely high. Immediately, the physician suspected a stroke. Dr. James Paullin, an internist from Atlanta, was called in. Paullin's medical report, filed later, stated:

> The President was [near death] when I reached him. He was in a cold sweat, ashy gray, and breathing with difficulty. . . . He was propped up in bed. His pupils were dilated and his hands slightly cyanosed. Commander Bruenn had already started artificial respiration. On examination, his pulse was barely perceptible.

The announcement that Roosevelt's inner circle of friends knew was inevitable came at 3:35 p.m. on April 12. After Doctors Paullin and Bruenn both listened with a stethoscope, trying feverishly to pick up FDR's heart sounds, they backed away from the bed and nodded to each other. "This man is dead," declared Dr. Bruenn as he closed the president's eyelids. Before the president's demise was made public, Lucy Rutherford was persuaded to leave the Little White House and driven to her home in South Carolina. When the news of the president's death was made public, no mention was made of the fact that Lucy had been present at the Little White House that day.

Mrs. Roosevelt flew down from Washington, DC, to bring her husband's body back to the capital. On April 13, at 10:13 a.m. Georgia time, the train carrying FDR's corpse left Warm Springs amid hundreds of crying residents and onlookers. Somewhere between Warm Springs and Atlanta, Eleanor learned from one of FDR's cousins that Lucy Rutherford had visited the president on the day of his death. Eleanor was extremely angry but kept her decorum throughout the funeral preparations and ceremonies.

Following the funeral in Washington, DC, President Roosevelt's body was transported to his family home in Hyde Park, New York, where he was laid to rest. He had asked that the stone over his grave be of white marble containing the inscription, "Franklin Delano Roosevelt 1882–19—." His wishes were carried out. In 1997, the multimillion-dollar Franklin D. Roosevelt Memorial was formally dedicated in the Tidal Basin in Washington, DC.

FRANK YERBY

[1916–1991]

When Frank Yerby died in Spain in November of 1991, the *New York Times* called the seventy-six-year-old Augusta native "one of the most popular writers in the United States in the 1940s and '50s." Over his lifetime, he published more than thirty books, which sold more than fifty million copies.

As a young student in local schools, Yerby expressed an early interest in literature, and by his seventeenth birthday, he had already published some of his poems. He graduated from historically black Paine College, a Methodist school in Augusta, and then earned his master's degree from Fisk University in Nashville. After Fisk, he furthered his education at the University of Chicago and gained valuable experience by working on the Federal Writers Project, launched by President Franklin D. Roosevelt during the Great Depression to employ librarians, writers, and others.

Leaving Chicago, Yerby taught English before moving to Michigan to work for Ford Motor Company. By 1944, he was working for Ranger Aircraft in New York. About that time, he submitted a short story to *Harper's Magazine*

that was readily published and earned him an O. Henry Award. He gained national attention and acclaim in 1946 upon the publication of *The Foxes of Harrow*, which told of an illegitimate Irishman who made his way to antebellum New Orleans, won a plantation in a gambling contest, then fought to keep it and the woman he loved. During the first year of publication, the blockbuster sold over one million copies and was optioned to Hollywood, where the movie of the same title was made starring Rex Harrison, Maureen O'Hara, and Richard Haydn. According to the online New Georgia Encyclopedia, "He was the first African American to write a series of best-selling novels and to have a book purchased by a Hollywood studio for a film adaptation."

Yerby's phenomenal success with *The Foxes of Harrow* was quickly followed up with *The Golden Hawk* in 1948, *A Woman Called Fancy* in 1951, and *The Saracen Blade* in 1952. Yerby spent his final years in France and Spain. His last novel, *McKenzie's Hundred*, was released in 1986.

1947

Three-Governor
Controversy

"The court of last resort is the people of Georgia. This case will be taken to the court of last resort," proclaimed Herman Talmadge to reporters after vacating the Georgia governor's mansion in March 1947 after a brief sixty-day tenure. The bizarre series of events preceding his pronouncement represents a constitutional crisis unlike any other in state politics. While Georgians debated their new Constitution of 1945, the national press focused its attention on the polarization of the Old South political machine versus the New South reform movement.

Veteran Georgia politician Eugene Talmadge was suffering from cirrhosis of the liver during the November 1947 general election. Despite this, when the election was over, he had been reelected governor for the fourth (nonconsecutive) time. Aware of his illness, many of Talmadge's supporters had written in the name of Eugene's son, Herman, who had worked on his father's campaigns and was well acquainted with the Talmadge political machine.

Also during the November 1947 election, anti-Talmadge politician Melvin Thompson had been elected lieutenant governor of Georgia, an office newly created by Georgia's Constitution of 1945. The constitution stated that the lieutenant governor would become acting governor in the case of the governor's death. Unfortunately, the Constitution of 1945 did not explain who should take over if the governor-elect died before taking office.

Outgoing governor Ellis Arnall, also an anti-Talmadge politician, refused to relinquish the governorship until the Georgia Supreme Court made its decision concerning what should be done if the governor-elect died before taking office. He pointed to the portion of the constitution requiring the outgoing governor to remain in office "until his successor shall be chosen and qualified" and insisted that he would surrender the office only to lieutenant governor Thompson, whom he considered the rightful heir. It seemed inevitable that Herman Talmadge, Thompson, and Arnall would square off over the issue.

All speculation became reality when Eugene Talmadge died on December 21, 1947. As he lay in the state capitol, more than ten thousand mourners passed his casket in less than six hours, and flags were flown half-mast. It was then that the constitutional crisis began to unfurl. Three interpretations of the new constitution were presented: the incumbent governor should govern until his successor was chosen (favored by Arnall); the lieutenant-governor should govern (Thompson's claim); or the General Assembly should choose the successor from the persons receiving the second majority of votes in the previous election (Talmadge's argument).

Governor Arnall asked the Georgia attorney general for an opinion on the matter, and it was ruled that Arnall had claim to the office until Thompson was sworn in. On January 11, 1948, Arnall announced that he would resign as soon as Thompson was sworn in as lieutenant governor.

However, the General Assembly, strongly supported by Talmadge backers, decided that Thompson did not rightfully deserve to be governor since he had not been sworn in as lieutenant governor before Eugene Talmadge died. The events that followed beckoned chaos.

In anticipation of Arnall's resignation, Melvin Thompson set up his headquarters in the office of the President of the Senate. Supported by the General Assembly, Herman Talmadge moved into the office of the Speaker of the House. A reported two to three thousand Talmadge supporters swarmed the capitol, and according to Talmadge, were served "drinks laced with knock-out drops" by Thompson backers. After unconscious legislators were revived and unauthorized visitors cleared from the gallery, the General Assembly decided to choose the next governor from the next two gubernatorial candidates receiving the most votes in the November 1947 election. When the votes were counted, to everyone's surprise, Herman Talmadge had only come in third among write-in votes.

The Telfair County delegation, ironically Talmadge's home county, immediately recounted their votes. When the count was rechecked, an envelope containing fifty-eight additional Telfair County votes was found. It was mislabeled as containing ballots for lieutenant governor, rather than governor. These write-in ballots made Herman Talmadge one of the top candidates after Eugene Talmadge. It was later discovered that all of the Telfair ballots were written in the same handwriting, were in alphabetical order, and included "constituents" residing in the local Telfair county cemeteries. Herman Talmadge denied any knowledge of how he came to have votes by deceased voters. Remarkably, the matter was ignored, the General Assembly voted, and Herman was declared the governor of Georgia.

In anticipation of possible violence, major radio networks sent war correspondents to cover the events unfolding at the Georgia capitol. *Newsweek* described the scene at the time: "The Talmadge crowd—the poor white farmers, crossroads grocers and 'wool-hat boys' from the sticks—brought a carnival air to Atlanta's staid graystone Capitol. They wanted to tromp in and put their shoes on desks and break out into Rebel yells now and then. And now they made the most of their chance."

Moreover, the National Guard, which was filled with ardent Talmadge supporters, had recently returned from active duty in World War II. While the National Guard was overseas, the State Patrol, loyal to Arnall and Thompson, had been formed as a replacement. Since the State Patrol had not yet been disbanded when the National Guard returned, it was feared that violence would erupt between these two armies. Though the National Guard seized the desk of Arnall's receptionist and secretary after Herman Talmadge's swearing in on January 15, Ellis Arnall refused to relinquish the governor's office to a "pretender."

For the next few days, both Talmadge and Arnall performed gubernatorial duties. Talmadge, occupying Arnall's executive secretary's office, made appointments. Arnall, who had moved to a nearby law office, swore in judges. After

Arnall left his office one evening, Talmadge ordered the locks changed in the governor's office. The following morning Arnall pushed through Talmadge supporters on his way to the governor's reception room, only to be barred from entering by a newly appointed secretary. Enraged, Arnall left the suite and set up his new office in the rotunda's information booth. Talmadge was quoted as saying, "I understand he's [Arnall] holding down the bathroom in the basement now."

On January 18, Arnall finally resigned the governorship on his own authority in favor of Thompson. Thompson took the oath of acting governor, went to Talmadge's office, and demanded Talmadge vacate the office. Talmadge refused, thus causing a political schism. The power struggle that followed became so intense that Secretary of State Ben Fortson removed the state seal from its safe and kept it until the matter was resolved. The state seal was a stamp that made government documents official, and Fortson feared that it would be misused if it fell into the hands of Thompson, Talmadge, or Arnall.

The three-governor controversy finally reached the Georgia Supreme Court. The court ruled that the General Assembly should have declared Eugene Talmadge the governor-elect. When Eugene died, Melvin Thompson should have been sworn in as governor because the declared governor-elect was deceased. More importantly, the court ruled that a special election should be held in 1948 to decide who should serve as governor for the remainder of Eugene Talmadge's term. Herman Talmadge finally did vacate his office after this ruling, relinquishing governorship to Thompson, but he proceeded to toss his hat into the 1948 special election. Talmadge defeated Thompson in the special election of 1948 and served as governor of Georgia from 1949 to 1955.

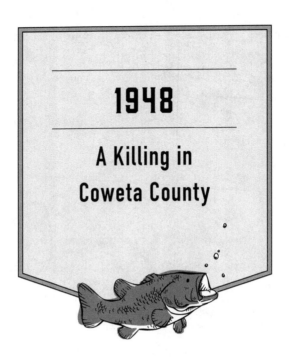

1948

A Killing in
Coweta County

Sometime in November, 1945, William Turner, a recent
deserter from the US Army, approached John Wallace,
well-known Meriwether County farmer, cattleman, milk
producer—and longtime moonshiner on the side—for a job.
Wallace agreed to hire Turner as a sharecropper and farm
worker, furnishing the young man, his wife, and baby son
with a nice house in which he and his mother had lived when
he returned from college in 1916.

The relationship between the two men got off to a good
start. Turner was eager to learn all he could about farming,
livestock, gardening, and all of the other facets of agriculture
that might one day make him as successful as his new boss.
He was also interested in the business of moonshining. Wallace—previously convicted in 1928 and again in 1934 for

making illegal whiskey—had spent time in the federal penitentiary in Atlanta, and was willing to share his knowledge. After Turner made a handsome profit from his 1946 cotton crop, he persuaded Wallace to increase his holdings. Wallace obliged, and issued 100 acres and a tractor to the happy sharecropper.

> The state fish is the largemouth bass (Microproterus salmoides).

Wallace was glad to have a competent person assisting him in his day-to-day farming activities, and maybe thought of Turner like the son he never had, but somewhere along the way, the relationship turned sour. Wallace had always been keenly interested in cattle. He had a fine herd of Guernseys, which, according to Dot Moore, the author of a book about Wallace, "were gentle, easy to breed and to give birth, and ... gave more golden milk than had been seen locally before. The Guernsey milk was also easily made into cheese, butter, and ice cream." Wallace had once boasted that he had paid more than $3,000 for one of his prize cows, nearly $50,000 in today's economy. He was well-known all over the region and, in present-day jargon, he practically "owned" Meriwether County, including many public officials. He was personable, well-educated, a good businessman, and had an honorable discharge from the US Army, but he could also be hotheaded, ruthless, and apparently, quick to kill. According to Elzie J. Hancock, the head agent for the Bureau of Internal Revenue's Columbus, Georgia, office, "[M]oonshiners ... didn't mind shooting and they didn't mind who they shot." About Wallace specifically, he once stated, "John Wallace [thought] that if a man needed killing, that was reason enough." Wallace himself admitted to Sheriff Lamar Potts of Coweta County that over his lifetime, he had killed four men, adding that "They all needed it."

The relationship between Wallace and Turner began to deteriorate in early 1947. Wallace, who had found out that Turner had "resumed his liquor operations," strongly urged Turner to "discontinue the practice, but to no avail." (This in itself seems strange, since Wallace had been moonshining on his own property for years, unless, based upon his own experiences, he was truly trying to keep the younger man out of trouble.)

In any event, Wallace blew the whistle on Turner and reported his newfound knowledge to authorities, even leading them to the locations of the stills where the illicit whiskey was being made. When Wallace discovered that Turner was using some of his black farm helpers to assist in his distilling operations, Wallace "called him and gave him specific orders to discontinue the practice." Apparently, during this time, according to Wallace, Turner made death threats upon his life. For whatever reason, Turner was never arrested.

As the winter of 1947–48 rolled around, John Wallace learned that a number of his cattle had disappeared. "I searched high and low for the cattle, never thinking that Turner was responsible," Wallace wrote. He contacted law enforcement authorities who monitored the auction and cattle sales houses in the region. At last, one of the prized cows was found in nearby Carrollton. Wallace drove to Carrollton, identified the cow as his property, and "became convinced that Turner was responsible." Several days later, the Carrollton chief of police arrested Turner attempting to take the cow from its holding pen. Turner was returned to Greenville, the county seat of Meriwether County, where he was jailed, charged, and then released at noon on Tuesday, April 20, 1948.

To sort out what happened next is something of a quandary, as several conflicting versions have been passed down over the years. However, one aspect of the incident that followed is fairly certain. When Turner left the Meriwether County Jail, he was pursued by Wallace and Herring Sivell in one car. Two additional Wallace associates, Henry Mobley and Tom Strickland, were to follow in a second car, but for some reason, they were delayed and did not really figure into the episode that was to follow until later.

Turner headed north in his pickup truck on State Highway 41, speeding toward the Coweta County line. For 17 miles the two vehicles raced along the narrow, rural, two-lane road until they crossed into Coweta County, Turner still in the lead. Then, Turner's pickup ran out of gas just as it neared the hamlet of Moreland. The chief attraction in Moreland was the Sunset Tourist Camp, which featured overnight accommodations, a cafe, and a gasoline pump.

Screeching to a stop in front of the camp, Turner ran toward the cafe but failed to get there before Wallace and Sivell had grabbed him from behind and dragged him toward their automobile. Turner was fighting fiercely to prevent from being forced into the backseat of the car when Wallace struck him in the head with a shotgun. (Wallace later testified that the blow to the head had only caused a minor cut.) In any event, Wallace and Sivell jammed Turner into the backseat and sped off southward, back toward Greenville.

A few miles down the road, a tire on the Wallace vehicle went flat. When Wallace's two other associates in the second car caught up with them, Turner was transferred to that car, supposedly under his own power and unassisted. Wallace shifted to that car as well and ordered the driver to continue. Sivell, the driver of the car with the flat tire, told his wife that evening, "Well, John did get mad and I think he got us into some big trouble, even though he promised us he was not going to do that. Big trouble." Over the next several days, no one heard from Turner, and his wife reported him missing.

Sheriff Lamar Potts, the no-nonsense chief law enforcement official in Coweta County, took charge of the investigation. He assembled two hundred men to perform an intensive search for Turner, including officers from the Georgia Highway Patrol and the State Bureau of Revenue. The local newspaper ran a photograph and an article about the missing man.

> William Turner . . . who was last seen Tuesday afternoon, just after noon, at the Sunset Tourist Camp, where he was reportedly assaulted by two men, thrown into the rear of a green two-door Ford, and carried away in a southward direction on Highway 41, presumably heading toward Greenville. $500 reward for information leading to his recovery.

When results were not forthcoming, Sheriff Potts made a gutsy decision. He personally called John Wallace and asked him if he and Herring Sivell would mind dropping by his office in the Coweta County Courthouse at Newnan, the county seat, to discuss the possible fate of William Turner. When the two men and their lawyer entered the sheriff's office, Potts handcuffed Wallace and Sivell and charged them with kidnapping, since at this point no one knew whether Turner was dead or alive, and placed them in jail. Eventually Strickland and Mobley were arrested and charged, as well.

With his primary suspects in William Turner's disappearance now behind bars, Sheriff Potts did his due diligence and investigated the crime with a passion. A search of Wallace's home revealed clothes soaked with human blood in the laundry basket. Two of Wallace's farmhands were later interrogated and revealed that their employer had ordered them to search for "a package" in a number of water wells located on his property. Following hours of trying to find the mysterious package, which supposedly held Turner's corpse, they finally succeeded and pulled it out of one of the wells with a grappling hook. The two frightened men then told the sheriff that Wallace told them to build a massive fire and place the package in the flames. At the site of the fire, authorities found the remains of a human body, largely unrecognizable. In a nearby creek, human bone fragments were also discovered. When this evidence was presented to the judge, he in turn presented it to a grand jury, which indicted Wallace and the others for murder.

Wallace's trial began on Monday, June 14, 1948, eight weeks after Turner had disappeared and was presumed dead. One hundred and nine potential jurors, all white males and mostly farmers, were called for jury duty—a rather large number, probably based on the assumption that many would object to capital punishment if Wallace was found guilty. As it turned out, not a single potential juror asked to be excused for that reason, most likely raising doubts in the defendants' minds about their future. In the meantime, Wallace's three associates, also charged with murder, had cut a deal with prosecutors: If they didn't testify on Wallace's behalf, they would not receive death penalties.

The five-day-long trial was rather mundane until the last day, when Wallace himself, over the objections of his lead attorney, testified on his own behalf. He had already confessed that he had killed Turner, but that it was an accident. Explaining the circumstances in a letter written later to the Georgia Board of Pardons and Paroles, Wallace explained that following his apprehension of Turner at the tourist camp, they returned to the scene of the cattle thefts, where he "had no intention to take [Turner's] life . . . when the gun accidentally fired, I did not know he had been struck until I turned around and found him dead. His scalp was blown off."

Wallace's disjointed, seven-hour testimony ranged from telling tales of his childhood to detailing his army service during World War I, to his life as a farmer and cattleman. But he never admitted murder in Turner's slaying, instead declaring that after the accidental killing, his "mind just went blank."

The jury adjourned at around 3:00 p.m., and before Wallace's lead attorney could walk down the street to his nearby hotel room, the jury had already returned its verdict—guilty—and the judge had pronounced the sentence—death by electrocution. Author Dot Moore writes that:

> The crowd and even the jury probably would have forgiven him for the murder, for murders and killings were fairly common. . . . It was the burning of Turner's body that was not forgivable. John Wallace was seeking to escape charges of murder by getting rid of his victim. . . . Then and now in that part of the country, the body of a deceased person is treated with sentiment and respect, and religious funerals are usually held. . . . But on June 18 when the trial was over, the mood of the jury, and of most of the crowd, was outrage. "An eye for an eye and a tooth for a tooth" was

a Bible verse that most knew and many had been raised to believe. John Wallace's "mind going blank" would determine the decision of the jury. He should have listened to [his attorney] and never gotten on the witness stand.

As the ensuing weeks turned into months and as the months turned into two and a half years, Wallace's lawyers filed appeal after appeal, all of which were denied. Stays of execution were granted several times, only delaying what Wallace must have known was the inevitable. While he waited in his prison cell with little more than time on his hands, he found religion. He stayed remarkably upbeat, telling one recipient of a letter that, "I shall rejoice when you all shall unite with me in a Land filled with love," and to another, "May we all get together in Heaven." He kept notes on blank pages in his Bible, one such reading, "Tom Strickland could have told the truth and possibly helped save my life."

On November 3, 1950, the day of his execution, Wallace was still denying that he had murdered William Turner. Among his final words were "I've still got my hopes. The good Lord will take care of me." He prayed for the "Governor and the Pardons and Paroles Board who didn't know the facts." And he told God, "I want to say before You, I am not guilty of this crime for which I am now paying the penalty." John Wallace died at 10:49 a.m.

A CBS television movie, *Murder in Coweta County*, based on the book of the same name by Margaret Anne Barnes, was released in 1983, starring Andy Griffith as John Wallace and Johnny Cash as Sheriff Lamar Potts.

1949

The Tragic Death of Margaret Mitchell

At a few minutes past eight o'clock during the evening of August 11, 1949, several people walking along Peachtree Street near its intersection with Thirteenth Street in Atlanta watched in horror as a speeding automobile suddenly swerved out of control. The driver of the car, a twenty-nine-year-old off-duty taxi driver, slammed on his brakes and veered left as he attempted to miss hitting two pedestrians crossing the busy downtown thoroughfare. One of the pedestrians, a petite woman in her late forties wearing a printed house dress, was too busy assisting her crippled husband to notice the rapidly approaching vehicle. When she heard the screeching brakes and looked to her right to see the car bearing down on them, she intuitively released her husband's arm, turned, and jumped backward—directly into the car's path.

When an ambulance arrived twelve minutes later, the woman was unconscious and bleeding profusely. Attendants loaded her onto a stretcher, assisted her shaken but uninjured husband into the vehicle with her, and sped off for Grady Hospital. It took emergency room physicians just a few minutes to determine that the lady suffered from a severe skull fracture, a concussion, massive internal injuries, and a fractured pelvis. Fearing that she could not survive an operation to relieve pressure on the brain, the doctors placed her in a private room and initiated an around-the-clock vigil.

In the meantime, the world was quickly learning the identity of the traffic victim. She was one of Atlanta's most famous and best loved figures, known to her fans as Margaret Mitchell. Mitchell's novel, *Gone With the Wind*, had become one of the most popular books ever written in the English language during its thirteen years of continuous publication. In addition to being awarded the Pulitzer Prize and selling millions of copies, the novel had been adapted by Hollywood into a blockbuster movie starring screen idol Clark Gable and a relative newcomer to American audiences, Vivien Leigh, in the lead roles.

For the next four days, under the constant vigil of her husband, John Marsh, and her brother, Stephens Mitchell, Margaret lay in a coma, murmuring a word or two only on rare occasions. Hospital personnel were inundated with thousands of inquiries from well-wishers all over the world including a phone call from President Harry Truman. By the morning of August 16, the hospital's medical staff decided that they must operate on Margaret's brain, but before the surgery could be performed, she died.

In the following days and weeks, Margaret Mitchell was lionized by the nation's press as few women have ever been, before or since. The *Manchester Guardian* called her a "woman of courtesy, generosity and good sense," while the *New York Times* lamented that the "South and the Nation have lost one of their most beloved and admired personages," adding, "Certainly she will always be one of our most remarkable literary figures." In its December 25, 1949 issue, *Time* carried a brief, but informative obituary:

> Died Margaret Munnerlyn Mitchell Marsh, 49, author of the bestselling novel *Gone With the Wind*; of injuries suffered when she was run down by an automobile; in Atlanta. A one-time reporter for the *Atlanta Journal* (1922–26), diminutive (4 ft. 11 in.) Margaret Mitchell, bedridden and later on crutches after an accident in 1926, was prompted by her husband John Marsh to write a novel instead of straining her eyes reading them. She wrote off & on for nearly ten years, reluctantly surrendered her incomplete manuscript to the Macmillan Co. in 1935. The monumental (1,037 pages) Civil War romance was a spectacular success, sold more than 6,000,000 copies in 30 languages, earned for its publicity-shy author a Pulitzer Prize (1937) and well over $1,000,000.

A little more than a decade earlier and only a few blocks away from the site of her fatal accident, Margaret Mitchell had celebrated what was perhaps the most memorable event in her life. On December 15, 1939, the world premiere of the movie based on her novel was held at Loews Grand Theater located on Peachtree Street. In attendance were the governors from Georgia, South Carolina, Tennessee, Alabama, and Florida; Atlanta's mayor, William Hartsfield; and the elite of Atlanta's social set, not to mention most of the actors, including Clark Gable, Vivian Leigh, and Olivia de Havilland.

Atlanta's streets were lined with thousands of frantic onlookers anxious for a peek at Gable or Leigh. Temporary Grecian columns lined the facade of the theater, bringing an antebellum look to the otherwise plain building. Confederate flags waved and bands played "Dixie," all to the joy of the thousands of Georgians who braved the cold temperature to catch a glimpse of the gala affair. "Ermine to the right of us, to the left, front and rear," wrote a reporter for the *Atlanta Georgian* describing the scene inside the theater. "Top hats and tails . . . Silver foxes, sables, fabulous jewelry, orchids."

Just before the film was to be shown, Margaret was called upon to make a few remarks. She had always been a quiet, shy, and withdrawn person, but she squarely faced the challenge and on behalf of herself and the heroine of her book, Scarlett O'Hara, she said:

> I think everybody who knows me . . . knows that I am not a speaker, and so please excuse me if I stumble through what I am going to say. That is that I want to thank you, for me and my poor Scarlett, for all the grand things that everybody has done—the taxi drivers, the librarians, the bankers, the Junior League, the girls behind the counters, the boys in the filling stations. What could I have done—and my poor Scarlett—without their kindness and their helpfulness! You know everybody thinks it's just when you are dead broke and you are out of luck that you need friends. But really, when you've had as incredible success as I have had, that's really when you need friends. And, thank Heaven, I've had them. And I've

appreciated everything people have done for me, to be kind to me and my Scarlett.

Despite the tremendous esteem and the personal fortune that *Gone With the Wind*—the book and the movie—brought to Margaret Mitchell, she died an unhappy woman. Although she labored over her book for ten years—more than a quarter of her life when it was finally completed in early 1936—she never intended for it to be published. And, after it was, she continuously refused to take part in its success.

> *The state flower is the Cherokee rose (Rosa laevigata).*

Soon after the book was released, Margaret wrote to the president of her publishing company, Macmillan, confiding in him that her rapidly gained success had made a nightmare out of her life, and that, furthermore, she thought it was a shame with all of the money she was making that she didn't even have the time to buy a new dress!

Hollywood had expressed keen interest in *Gone With the Wind* from its infancy as a bestseller. But after Margaret struck a deal with movie mogul David O. Selznick, in which she was to receive a previously unheard-of $50,000 for the film rights, she steadfastly refused to take any part in the creation, production, or publicity of the film.

Despite all of the headaches that Mitchell suffered—real and perceived—she was very proud of the success of her book and the movie based upon it. *Gone With the Wind*, the book, remains one of the biggest bestsellers in world publishing history. And, although more-recent blockbusters have surpassed it in dollars received at the box office, *Gone With the Wind*, the movie—after figures are adjusted for inflation—continues to reign as the highest-grossing film of all time, according to several studies.

BRENDA LEE

[B. 1944]

In 1957, a young girl from Atlanta, Georgia, burst upon the Nashville music scene and began a career that was unprecedented for contemporary female popular singers. Brenda Lee, who became known as "Little Miss Dynamite," could burst out a song that brought audiences to their feet. The future international teen idol was born in Atlanta. She won a talent show when she was only five years old, and soon found herself singing on local radio shows and the new medium of television. Her family moved to Augusta in 1955, where she continued her singing, sometimes sharing the spotlight with Augusta native Wyche Fowler, who later became a US congressman, senator, and ambassador to Saudi Arabia.

The young performer, born Brenda Mae Tarpley, soon changed her name to "Brenda Lee," following the advice of a TV producer. In Augusta, in 1956, she sang Hank Williams's popular "Jambalaya" in company with the legendary country-and-western singer Red Foley, and he asked Lee to join his nationally viewed *Ozark Jubilee* TV show. By the time she reached Nashville the following year, her popularity and future in the music industry were assured.

In 1958, Lee released "Rockin' Around the Christmas Tree," an overwhelming success that sold over twenty-five million copies. "Sweet Nothin's," released in 1960, was among the top five songs that year in both the United States and Great Britain. Her most popular song, "I'm Sorry," was also released in 1960. For the next decade, Lee was immensely popular in the United States as well as in Japan, Great Britain, and Germany. For the period, her records hit *Billboard*'s country, pop, adult contemporary, and rhythm-and-blues charts fifty-five times, and she reigned as the fourth-most-popular singer, led only by Elvis Presley, the Beatles, and Ray Charles. She is a member of both the Rock & Roll and the Country Music Halls of Fame, and has received a Grammy Award for Lifetime Achievement. More than 100 million of her records have sold worldwide.

1966

The Metcalf Stone

Manfred Metcalf was beginning to feel a little weary as he sorted through the large limestone blocks that sprawled before him. As he piled one rock after another into the heap, he wondered if it was really worth building his outdoor fireplace with these stones from the old deserted gristmill located on the Fort Benning Military Reservation near Columbus, Georgia.

When he arrived home on that evening during the summer of 1966, Metcalf deposited his new batch of stones in the backyard, adding to the large pile that he had already gathered from various places across the countryside. Satisfied that he now had enough stones to build a handsome fireplace on his patio, Metcalf contemplated when he might find the time from his busy schedule to devote to the actual construction project.

As autumn approached, Metcalf decided to begin work on the fireplace. Searching through the pile of stones, looking for pieces that would be suitable for various parts of the structure, he came upon one medium-sized rock that was covered with curious markings. Metcalf was an amateur archaeologist and historian, and he was quick to appreciate the importance of the crude scratches that, over the years, had become almost invisible. As he carefully washed away the dirt and moss that covered the stone, he became excited by what his efforts uncovered. It was perfectly clear to him that the markings were not natural but, rather, that they had been purposefully engraved in the rock's surface by humans.

Metcalf conferred with a local geologist who helped him determine the stone's origin. The geologist told Metcalf that the rock, comprised of red sandstone, was most likely one of those that he had picked up at the Fort Benning mill site. The two men returned to the mill and carefully scoured the area for more rocks with the strange markings, but after a great deal of searching, they found no others. They agreed that since the mill had been built in the nineteenth century, and the stone had been one used in its construction, that it had probably lain for years, undisturbed, in the spot where Metcalf had found it.

In September Metcalf loaded the stone into his car and drove to nearby Columbus, where he met with Professor Joseph B. Mahan Jr., an experienced ethnologist and archaeologist and the director of education and research at the Columbus Museum of Arts and Crafts. Coincidentally, Mahan had only recently been researching the astounding similarities between rituals of the Yuchi Indians, a tribe that inhabited northern Georgia and neighboring Tennessee when white settlers first arrived, and those of the ancient

Hebrews and other Bronze Age peoples of the eastern Mediterranean Sea region. When Metcalf showed his glyph-inscribed stone to him, Mahan immediately recognized that the strange markings resembled Near Eastern writing systems from the second century BC.

After carefully examining the Metcalf Stone, as the rock was eventually called, Mahan was convinced that it was real and had not been engraved recently. The scientist had a plaster cast of the stone made and shipped it off to Professor Cyrus H. Gordon, head of the Department of Mediterranean Studies at Brandeis University in Massachusetts. Gordon was one of the foremost authorities on Middle Eastern and Mediterranean history and prehistory, and one of his fields of expertise was the decipherment and translation of ancient writings.

Gordon studied the plaster cast of the Metcalf Stone intensely, and eventually made a trip to Columbus to view the original at the museum and to con-fer with Professor Mahan. Pooling their joint knowledge and expertise, the two scientists became convinced that the glyph-engraved rock was positive evidence that the prehistoric Indians of Georgia and much of the southeastern United States were somehow linked to the people and cultures of the East-ern Mediterranean Sea during the Bronze Age. According to Gordon and Mahan, the Metcalf Stone gave hard proof that seafaring Bronze Age peoples sailed across the Atlantic Ocean in the dim days of early Old Testament history and colonized parts of Georgia and other locales throughout the southeastern United States.

Mahan and Gordon were not the first to suspect a connection between the Old World and the New World during the centuries before Columbus discovered America. For example, James Adair, a well-educated Scots-Irish trader who did business with the Chickasaw, Choctaw, Cherokee, and Creek Indians of the southeast, and who traveled extensively throughout Georgia, believed that all of these tribes were descended from the Jews. In his extremely well-documented book for the times, *The History of the American Indians*, published in London in 1775, Adair tried to convert his readers to his way of thinking. He wrote:

> From the most exact observations I could make in the long time I traded with the Indian Americans, I was forced to believe them lineally descended from the Israelites, either while they were a maritime power, or soon after the general captivity; the latter however is the most probable. This descent, I shall endeavor to prove from their religious rites, civil and martial customs, their marriages, funeral ceremonies, manners, language, traditions, and a variety of particulars.

Two hundred and twenty pages later, in his closing arguments, Adair wrote:

> I presume, enough hath been said to point out the similarity between the rites and customs of the native American Indians, and those of the Israelites [and] that the Indian system is derived from the moral, ceremonial, and judicial laws of the Hebrews, though now but a faint copy of the divine original. Their religious rites, martial customs, dress, music, dances,

and domestic forms of life, seem clearly to evince also, that they came to America in early times.

Today, no one but the Mormons seriously believes that American Indians descended from the Ten Lost Tribes of Israel or from any other Jewish or Near Eastern civilization, as James Adair speculated. However, with each succeeding decade, more and more evidence appears that would seem to indicate a strong connection between the natives of the New World and those of the European and Asiatic Bronze Age. As Cyrus Gordon explains in his book *Before Columbus*:

> Neither Mahan nor I believe that the Yuchis are "one of the Ten Lost Tribes," nor is there any evidence showing that they stem from any segment of the Jewish people. It is, rather, our view that both the Yuchis and the ancient Hebrews share certain cultural features rooted in the same ancient East Mediterranean of the Bronze Age.

1974

Breaking the Babe's Home-Run Record

By the time darkness crept across the Georgia landscape on Monday, April 8, 1974, ominous storm clouds were moving in on Atlanta Stadium. But the menacing rains did not stop the city's avid baseball fans as nearly fifty-four thousand of them—the largest crowd ever to attend a baseball game in Atlanta—poured through the gates and anxiously sought their seats beneath the bright lights that illuminated the field. This was the Atlanta Braves' first home game of the 1974 season, and everyone in the crowd knew this was a game that might make baseball history.

Hank Aaron was apprehensive, if not nervous. The forty-year-old Braves outfielder wondered if tonight might be the night when he would hit his 715th home run. If so, he would pass Babe Ruth's 1935 record of 714 home runs. Only a few days earlier, in Cincinnati's Riverfront Stadium, during the first ball game of the new season, Aaron had tied Ruth's long-held record with a powerful hit that carried the ball 400 feet over the left field wall. The 52,154 fans in the crowd gave Aaron, who was beginning his twenty-first year in major league baseball, a standing ovation as the ball went soaring out of the park.

In Atlanta as Aaron had requested, his father Herbert, a boilermaker's assistant from Mobile, Alabama, threw out the first pitch, and the Braves' game against the Los Angeles Dodgers was under way. The Braves quickly retired the Dodgers in the top of the first inning, and the Dodgers returned the favor in the bottom of the first. When Aaron's turn at bat came in the bottom of the second inning, the Dodgers' pitcher, veteran Al Downing, walked him. Dusty Baker then hit a double, and Aaron speedily rounded the bases to score. With that scored run, Aaron passed up Willie Mayes's National League record for runs scored, and landed in third place, behind Ty Cobb and Babe Ruth.

Aaron's next time at bat came in the fourth inning. As he came out of the dugout and neared Darrell Evans who was limbering up in the on-deck circle, he murmured, "I'm gonna get it over right now." Evans got to first base, there were two outs, and the Dodgers were leading with a score of three to one. Aaron stepped into the batter's box, and Downing, who traditionally threw him either sliders or screwballs, changed his pace on the first pitch, and the ball went spinning wildly into the dirt.

The home plate umpire retired the ball, as the first base umpire threw a new one out to Downing. For this game, the first base umpire maintained a supply of specially prepared baseballs that were used whenever Aaron was at bat. The balls had infrared markings on them so that, if and when Aaron hit his record-breaking 715th home run, there would be only one genuine baseball that could be claimed as the record-setter.

Downing's second pitch was a slider, low and dead center across home plate. Aaron swung and connected and watched as the slowing rising line drive sped over the shortstop's head. The Dodgers' outfielder made a mad dash toward the wall and, for a moment, it appeared that he was going to snag the ball. But, as Aaron wrote in his autobiography, by the time he got to first base, he knew that the baseball was gone and that he "was the all-time home run king of baseball."

> *The state tree is the live oak (*Quercus myrtifolia*).*

The crowd went wild. The Braves' dugout emptied in mere seconds as Aaron's teammates quickly gathered at home plate to congratulate him. Even the Dodgers got involved. First baseman Steve Garvey grabbed Aaron's hand when he passed first base. Davey Lopes, playing second base, did likewise, as did shortstop Bill Russell. As Aaron rounded third base, two University of Georgia students, who somehow bypassed the heavy security on the field, ran out onto the diamond and accompanied him to home plate. Hank recalled the magical moment in his autobiography:

> I was in my own little world at this time. It was like
> I was running in a bubble and I could see all these
> people jumping up and down and waving their arms

in slow motion. I remember that every base seemed crowded, like there were all these people I had to get through to make it to home plate. I just couldn't wait to get there. I was told I had a big smile on my face as I came around third. I purposely never smiled as I ran the bases after a home run, but I suppose I couldn't help it that time.

One of the most enthusiastic people gathered around home plate was Hank's mother Estella. "Somehow, my mother managed to make it through and put a bear hug on me," Aaron wrote later. "Good Lord, I didn't know Mama was that strong."

As the deafening roar from the crowd reverberated throughout Atlanta Stadium, it began to rain, and many of the spectators left. For a while, it appeared that the game might be called, but a later clearing allowed it to go on. The final score was seven to four in favor of the Braves.

In an ironic twist of fate, Aaron was traded to the Milwaukee Brewers the following season. After all, it was in Milwaukee when the team still carried the Braves name that Hank had begun his major league career in 1954. When the Braves moved to Atlanta at the end of the 1965 season, Aaron moved with them, but he had always maintained a special place in his heart for the fans in Milwaukee. Aaron played for the Brewers for two years after he broke the home-run record. He finally retired from professional baseball at the end of the 1976 season.

Hank Aaron's statistics are impressive. During his twenty-two years in the major leagues, he played a total of 3,298 record games, was at bat 12,364 times, had 3,771 hits, scored a record 2,174 times, batted in a record 2,297 runs, and had a lifetime batting average of .305. He finished his career with 755 home runs. He led the National League in runs batted in for the years 1957, 1960, 1963, and 1966. Likewise, he led the National League with home runs for the years 1957 (44), 1963 (44), 1966 (44), and 1967 (39). He had the highest batting average in the National League for 1956 (.328) and 1959 (.355).

When Aaron retired from the Milwaukee Brewers at the end of the 1976 season, he and his family returned to Atlanta, where he took a front-office position with the Braves as director of player development. Media mogul Ted Turner had just purchased the team, and under his administration, Hank Aaron eventually became vice president of the organization. In 1982 he was elected to the Baseball Hall of Fame in Cooperstown, New York. All but nine sports writers cast their votes for him. But, as Aaron explained in his casual style, "It didn't upset me, because eleven writers hadn't voted for Babe Ruth, and forty-three for Mickey Mantle."

CLARENCE THOMAS

[B. 1948]

At the time of his swearing-in, Clarence Thomas was not only the youngest US Supreme Court justice ever to sit on the bench, but also only the second African American to serve in that capacity. Clarence Thomas, a native of Pin Point, Georgia—a small village situated on a former antebellum plantation near Savannah, and home to primarily poor black families—fully intended as a youth to become a priest. In 1967, following his early education in local Catholic schools, he enrolled in a seminary in Missouri. As the only African American in his class, he often found himself a victim of racial prejudice. The end of his tolerance came when he overheard a seminary student extolling the assassination of Dr. Martin Luther King Jr. Thomas left the seminary and enrolled in Holy Cross College in Massachusetts, graduating in 1971 with high honors and a degree in English. From Holy Cross, he entered Yale Law School as part of the affirmative action program.

With his new law degree, Thomas returned to Missouri to work on the staff of the state attorney general, John Danforth, who soon afterwards was elected to the US Senate. Thomas rejoined Danforth in Washington, DC, in 1979 as an energy and environmental specialist. President Ronald Reagan chose Thomas as his assistant secretary of the Department of Education, then advanced him to chairman of the Equal Employment Opportunity Commission (EEOC). There, he was criticized by his foes for strongly supporting the administration's resistance to affirmative action. President George H. W. Bush selected Thomas to sit on the US Court of Appeals for the DC circuit. In late 1991, the US Senate confirmed Thomas's appointment to the US Supreme Court, replacing Justice Thurgood Marshall, the court's first black member.

Over the years, Thomas's opinions from the bench have often tended to fuel the ire of many liberal observers. One of his biographers, John P. Vanzo, writes that "In recent years he has adopted a more assertive, conservative, and consistent approach to constitutional interpretation that sets him apart."

1994

The Flood of 1994

As his plane descended from the clouds over Albany, Georgia, President Bill Clinton peered over the muddy waters of the Flint River that had ravaged the area's homes, churches, and businesses. Even before stopping at a disaster relief center, the president pledged $60 million in federal disaster aid to help the residents of Georgia, Alabama, and Florida affected by one of the worst storms to ever hit the southeastern United States. Meteorologists described the storm as a freak occurrence caused when tropical storm Alberto traveled up from the Gulf of Mexico to Atlanta then suddenly reversed its direction and stalled over Georgia and Florida on Sunday, July 3, 1994, and began dumping torrential rains. The area along the Flint River that starts near Atlanta and flows southwest into Lake Seminole at the

Georgia-Florida border, sustained the greatest devastation in the flood that followed.

The Macon to Americus corridor was the hardest hit with more than 16 inches of rain falling in Macon and a monstrous 27.61 inches falling in Americus. When Georgia governor Zell Miller toured the area early that week, some 10,000 square miles (an area the size of Massachusetts and Rhode Island combined) were under water. Forty thousand residents were temporarily homeless. Sixty thousand acres of peanuts, 19,000 acres of cotton, and 10,000 acres of corn were lost.

By Thursday the Ocmulgee River had risen high enough to cover three heavily traveled highways in the Macon area. The flood isolated the city of Macon, turning it into a virtual island. It was difficult to manage the rising floodwaters and Macon residents had no electricity or water. The central park area of the city had to be evacuated when a levee cracked. The National Guard used helicopters to rescue people from flooded areas in rural Macon while military police directed traffic to the roads that were passable.

As the rain continued to fall, factories were shut down while employees hurriedly moved inventory to higher ground. Downtown business was at a halt. Martin Willis, who operated the Best Western Riverside Inn in downtown Macon, remarked, "First, we had no power and no water. Now we got power back on but no water. The water shortage shut me down completely." To top it all off, a foul smell permeated rural Macon County for days after 250,000 chickens drowned. National Guardsmen had to wear masks when picking up the rotting carcasses.

Unfortunately, there was more trouble farther downstream. In Americus, where 21 inches of rain fell within twenty-four hours, sixteen people had perished in the floodwaters and several more were reported missing. Roads going into and out of the town had to be closed. In Americus's sister city of Albany, a dusk-to-dawn curfew was enforced to prevent looting. When the rain finally gave way to sunshine on Friday, July 8, fifteen thousand Albany residents were cautioned by authorities not to return to their homes until they had been inspected for water moccasins or alligators, which "may have taken a liking to suburban living."

Floodwaters caused coffins from local Albany cemeteries to dislodge from the earth and float like fishing bobbins through city streets. While touring the area, Governor Miller remarked, "I will never forget seeing those caskets and how I first started to count them. And I got up into the twenties, and I got up into the thirties, and I got up into the forties, and I thought, 'Well, I can't count them all; there's just so many of them.'"

Residents of Bainbridge on the northern tip of Lake Seminole, braced for the worst as floodwaters rose. The National Weather Service predicted that the Flint River would crest at 45 feet sometime on Thursday. At least a third of the city's ten thousand residents evacuated their homes, and city officials waited nervously to see if a dike the National Guard had erected around the ammonia storage tank at a fertilizer plant would keep floodwaters away from the chemical. If the wall failed ammonia vapors could leak into the water or escape into the air and create an emergency situation. Fortunately, a drainage area called the "Big Slough" absorbed most of the floodwaters, keeping them away from the storage tank.

Aside from assisting with evacuations, there was not much flood victims could do except pitch in where needed. Sergeant Bob Pruitt brought a contingent of 150 volunteers from Moody Air Force Base to Albany's James Gray Civic

Center parking lot to pack sandbags. Though their intentions were well founded, their efforts seemed futile, since the basement of the Civic Center was already covered by 2 feet of water. Some isolated rural areas generated emergency plans of their own. Truck drivers in Putney donated their rigs to haul families and furniture away from rising waters.

The following Monday, the Flint River crested at a record 44 feet. The overflowing river cut Albany in two when it covered roads connecting the eastern and western sections of the city. Travel from one side of Albany to the other required a one-hundred-mile detour. One Albany resident, Bonnie Bonson, was caught on the opposite side of the city from her home. Since hotel rooms were scarce, her only refuge was a couch in a hotel lobby.

Students from Nancy Smith Elementary School in Albany, Texas, collected 28,000 pennies as a thoughtful contribution for flood victims in Albany, Georgia. In a way they were returning a favor. In 1978 when the Texas city was devastated by flooding following 30 inches of rain, Albany, Georgia, was among the first to send aid.

As floodwaters dissipated and the cleanup started, Georgians began the task of recovering from one of the worst floods in American history. The destruction caused by the Flood of 1994 has been compared to the destruction of General Sherman's Civil War March to the Sea campaign. All told 32 people were killed in Georgia, 8,763 homes were damaged, and 55 Georgia counties were declared disaster areas. Approximately 11,500 Georgians applied for federal disaster assistance. New city councilman Jack Henderson summed up the sentiment of most west-central Georgians when he said, "It's going to be a long time before things get back to normal around here."

1996

Tragedy at the Olympic Games

The previous few days had been a dream come true for most Georgians and for the citizens of Atlanta in particular. The years of planning by city officials to host the Summer Olympic Games had finally paid off, and now as the second full week of competition was soon to begin, crowds of native Georgians and visitors alike milled about Atlanta's new Centennial Olympic Park in an almost carnival atmosphere.

It was early on Saturday morning, July 27, 1996, as deafening rock music played by Jack Mack and the Heart Attack band sent vibrations through the park, when a security officer was summoned by concerned onlookers witnessing a brief scuffle between a few nearby youngsters. Straightening out the harmless encounter, the officer checked his watch and read that it was almost 1:30 a.m. As he turned to walk away from the stage area, the music still blaring, he noticed what appeared to be an unattended knapsack leaning against one of the audio towers that held the stage's speakers.

The presence of the bundle was immediate cause for alarm. Any unattended bag or bundle could be a bomb, so the security officer quickly notified police officials in the area. As he talked to them on his walkie-talkie, he hoped that the knapsack had been left by mistake just as the more than one hundred other unattended packages, bags, and satchels that security personnel had removed from the area in the previous seven days had been. As a precaution, however, upon the arrival of reinforcements, security began evacuating the area. The loud music and the festivities of thousands of people milling about the park made the task difficult.

The concerned officers made their way through the rowdy crowd, urging people to evacuate the area as rapidly as possible. Suddenly, a deafening roar, accompanied by flames and smoke, engulfed the hundreds of onlookers positioned in front of the stage where the band was still playing. Shrapnel from the explosion struck scores of people, and one of them, a forty-four-year-old school teacher from Albany, was killed outright. Another victim, a Turkish television cameraman on assignment, suffered a heart attack and died minutes later. In all, more than one hundred innocent spectators were injured by the homemade bomb that had been concealed in the knapsack.

Atlanta police, the FBI, and agents from the Bureau of Alcohol, Tobacco, and Firearms descended on Centennial Olympic Park. Local firemen and paramedics arrived by the scores. Exits to the area were immediately closed, and thousands of people were trapped in the park with no way to get home or to their hotels. Health professionals began the work of ministering to the wounded and transporting them to local hospitals. One of them sadly commented, "I've been in the fire department sixteen years, and I've never seen that many people that critically injured."

The state song is "Georgia on My Mind."

As the wee hours of Saturday morning wore on, search dogs and additional security forces were brought in as well as thousands of federal military personnel and Georgia National Guardsmen. Orders were issued to scour all forty of the Olympic venues that were spread over the greater Atlanta area for bombs. At 5:20 a.m. Francois Carrard, the director of the International Olympic Committee, announced that despite the horrible and tragic events that had just visited the Olympic complex, "The games will go on." When Atlantans awoke that morning and flipped on their radios and televisions to pick up the latest news, they were aghast at the events that had occurred in their proud city while they and millions of other Americans slept. Most of the athletes were unaware of what had occurred during the early morning hours since most had checked into their dormitories early Friday evening for a good night's rest.

The incident was a mystery to most who heard the news or read about the tragic occurrence in the morning newspaper. How could this have happened in Atlanta, which according to Olympic and city officials, had thousands of security people swarming all over the town? In order to protect the ten thousand athletes and the potential crowd of two million spectators, city government had recruited thirty thousand law enforcement officers from a variety of organizations as well as eleven thousand Georgia National Guardsmen and US military personnel, including army rangers, commandos, chemical and biological warfare specialists, nuclear search team members, and explosives experts. A reporter for *Time* wrote that "The Olympic Village is a virtual fortress: on

city streets, manhole covers have been welded down to prevent anyone from getting access to power lines."

The FBI soon released information that described an anonymous telephone call made from a pay phone located just a few feet away from the site of the explosion. The call had been completed about eighteen minutes before the blast, and the caller had warned security officials that an explosion would occur within the next thirty minutes. An all-out effort was initiated to find the bomber, and after thousands of man hours had been spent on the investigation by members of the Atlanta Police Department; the FBI; the Bureau of Alcohol, Tax and Firearms; Olympic Security; and others, an announcement was made that the prime suspect in the case was the security guard who had discovered the unattended knapsack in the first place.

For the next several weeks, the various law enforcement agencies involved with the investigation worked to strengthen their case against the accused security guard, who vigorously maintained that he was innocent of all charges. Authorities soon realized that their case against the guard just did not stack up. With each passing day, they came to realize that they did not have the Olympic bomber after all.

Finally, in late October, they concluded the guard was no longer a suspect, and the falsely accused man started to put the pieces of his life back together. This man's life and career were ruined because of those who rushed to find a perpetrator and who did not take the time to review the facts. He, like the others wounded in Centennial Park, will take a long time to recover. Years after the incident, the real culprit, a right-wing extremist and terrorist named Eric Robert Rudolph, was apprehended, tried, and sentenced to prison.

BIBLIOGRAPHY

Aaron, Hank, with Lonnie Wheeler. *I Had a Hammer: The Hank Aaron Story*. New York: HarperCollins, 1991.

Adair, James. *The History of the American Indians*. London: Edward and Charles Dilly, 1775.

America's Fascinating Indian Heritage. Pleasantville, NY: The Reader's Digest Association, 1978.

Bishop, Jim. *FDR's Last Year: April 1944–April 1945*. New York: William Morrow, 1974.

Boland, Frank Kells. *The First Anesthetic: The Story of Crawford Long*. Athens, GA.: University of Georgia Press, 1950.

Burns, James MacGregor. *Roosevelt: The Soldier of Freedom*. New York: Harcourt Brace Jovanovich, 1970.

Burns, Rebecca. "The Second Burning of Atlanta," *Atlanta* magazine (February 2017).

Bynum, Hartwell T. "Sherman's Expulsion of the Roswell Women in 1864." *The Georgia Historical Quarterly*, vol. LIV, no. 2. Savannah: The Georgia Historical Society, 1970.

Cahoon, Brad. "Brenda Lee (b. 1944)," New Georgia Encyclopedia, July 16, 2018, www.georgiaencyclopedia.org/articles/arts -culture/brenda-lee-b-1944, accessed July 24, 2018.

Coulter, E. Merton. "The Acadians in Georgia," *Georgia Historical Quarterly*, vol. XLVII, no. 1. Savannah: The Georgia Historical Society, 1963.

———. "When John Wesley Preached in Georgia," *Georgia Historical Quarterly*, vol. IX, no. 4. Savannah: The Georgia Historical Society, 1925.

Crutchfield, James A. *The Georgia Almanac and Book of Facts*. Nashville: Rutledge Hill Press, 1988.

Davis, William C. *Jefferson Davis: The Man and His Hour*. New York: HarperCollins Publishers, 1991.

Drewry, Jones M. "The Double-barreled Cannon of Athens, Georgia," *Georgia Historical Quarterly*, vol. XLVIII, no. 4. Savannah: The Georgia Historical Society, 1964.

Driggs, Ken. "There is No Law in Georgia for Mormons: The Joseph Standing Murder Case of 1879," *Georgia Historical Quarterly*, vol. LXXIII, no. 4. Savannah: The Georgia Historical Society, 1989.

Edwards, Anne. *Road to Tara: The Life of Margaret Mitchell*. New Haven, CT.: Ticknor & Fields, 1983.

Egan, Clifford L. "Fracas in Savannah: National Exasperation in Microcosm, 1811." *The Georgia Historical Quarterly*, vol. LIV, no. 1. Savannah: The Georgia Historical Society, 1970.

Eskew, Glenn T. "Johnny Mercer (1909–1976)," New Georgia Encyclopedia, November 1, 2016, www.georgiaencyclopedia .org/articles/arts-culture/johnny-mercer-1909-1976, accessed July 9, 2018.

Farr, Finis. *Margaret Mitchell of Atlanta*. New York: William Morrow, 1965.

Faust, Patricia L., ed. *Historical Times Illustrated Encyclopedia of the Civil War*. New York: Harper & Row, 1986.

Fleming, Berry, comp. *The First Half-Century of Augusta, Georgia*. Spartanburg, SC: The Reprint Company, 1974.

Frazier, Valerie. "Frank Yerby (1916–1991)," New Georgia Encyclopedia, June 7, 2018, www.georgiaencyclopedia.org/ articles/arts-culture/frank-yerby-1916-1991, accessed July 24, 2018.

Gardner, Gerald, and Harriet M. Gardner. *Pictorial History of* Gone With the Wind. New York: Bonanza Books, 1983.

Gordon, Arthur. "My Aunt Daisy Was the First Girl Scout." n.p., 1956.

Gordon, Cyrus H. *Before Columbus: Links Between the Old World and Ancient America.* New York: Crown Publishers, 1971.

Grimes, William. "Frank Yerby, Writer, 76, is Dead; Novels of the South Sold Millions," *New York Times,* January 8, 1992.

Harper's Pictorial History of the Civil War. New York: The Fairfax Press, 1977.

Hays, Wilma Pitchford. *Eli Whitney: Founder of Modern Industry.* New York: Franklin Watts, 1965.

Highlights in Girl Scouting 1912–1996. New York: Girl Scouts of the U.S.A., 1997.

Jahoda, Gloria. *The Trail of Tears.* New York: Wings Books, 1995.

Jenkins, Charles Francis. *Button Gwinnett: Signer of the Declaration of Independence.* Spartanburg, SC: The Reprint Company, 1974.

Johnson, Loch K. "Dean Rusk (1909–1994)," New Georgia Encyclopedia, August 26, 2013, www.georgiaencyclopedia.org/ articles/government-politics/dean-rusk-1909-1994, accessed July 19, 2018.

Kastner, Joseph. *A Species of Eternity.* New York: E. P. Dutton, 1978.

Lanier, Doris. "Oscar Wilde Tours Georgia: 1882," *Georgia Historical Quarterly,* vol. LXV, no. 4. Savannah: The Georgia Historical Society, 1981.

Lippman, Jr., Theo. *The Squire of Warm Springs: FDR in Georgia, 1924–1945.* Chicago: Playboy Press, 1977.

Long, E. B. *The Civil War Day by Day.* Garden City, NJ: Doubleday, 1971.

Mango, Karin. "Juliette Low: The Lady from Savannah," *Hearing/ Health Magazine.* Ingleside, TX: Hearing Health Magazine, 1995.

McBryde, Randall W. *The Historic "General."* Chattanooga, TN: MacGowan & Cooke, 1904.

Miles, Tiya. *The House on Diamond Hill: A Cherokee Plantation Story.* Chapel Hill: University of North Carolina Press, 2010.

Miller, Rod. *John Muir Magnificent Tramp.* New York: Forge, 2005.

Mixon, Wayne. "Erskine Caldwell (1903–1987)," New Georgia Encyclopedia, May 16, 2016, www.georgiaencyclopedia.org/articles/arts-culture/erskine-caldwell-1903-1987, accessed July 19, 2018.

Moore, Dot. *No Remorse: The Rise and Fall of John Wallace.* Montgomery, AL: NewSouth Books, 2011.

"Mother Mathilda Beasley," Georgia Historical Society, https://georgiahistory.com/education-outreach/online-exhibits/featured-historical-figures/mother-mathilda-beasley/, accessed August 12, 2018.

Muir, John. *A Thousand-Mile Walk to the Gulf.* Dunwoody, GA: Norman S. Berg, nd.

Newsweek. April 15, 1974.

Nelson, Megan Kate. "The Burning of Atlanta," *New York Times,* November 10, 2014.

Parker, David B. "Rebecca Latimer Felton (1835–1930)," New Georgia Encyclopedia, February 21, 2018, www.georgiaencyclopedia.org/articles/history-archaeology/rebecca-latimer-felton-1835-1930, accessed July 19, 2018.

Peake, Ora Brooks. *A History of the United States Indian Factory System, 1795–1822.* Denver: Sage Books, 1954.

Peterson, Larry. "Mother Mathilda Beasley: 'The Idol of the Poor,'" www.catholic365.com/article/5777/mother-mathilda-beasley-the-idol-of-the-poor.html, accessed August 12, 2018.

Reese, Trevor R. *Frederica: Colonial Fort and Town.* St. Simons Island, GA: Fort Frederica Association, 1969.

Robbins, Peggy. "God, Man, Woman, and the Wesleys," *American Heritage,* vol. 35, no. 3. New York: American Heritage Publishing Company, 1984.

Rodgers, Thomas G. "Colonials Collide at Bloody Marsh," *Military History Magazine*. Leesburg, VA: Cowles History Group, 1996.

Sykes, W. Stanley. *Essays on the First Hundred Years of Anaesthesia*. Park Ridge, IL: American Society of Anesthesiologists, 1982.

Tate, Allen. *Jefferson Davis: His Rise and Fall*. New York: Minton, Balch & Company, 1929.

Through Indian Eyes: The Untold Story of Native American Peoples. Pleasantville NY: The Reader's Digest Association, 1996.

Time. December 25, 1939; August 29, 1949; April 22, 1974; August 5, 1996.

"Ty Cobb," National Baseball Hall of Fame, http://baseballhall.org/ hall-of-famers/cobb-ty, accessed July 19, 2018.

U.S. News & World Report. August 5, 1996.

Vanzo, John P. "Clarence Thomas (b. 1948)," New Georgia Encyclopedia, August 26, 2013, www.georgiaencyclopedia.org/ articles/government-politics/clarence-thomas-b-1948, accessed July 19, 2018.

Williams, David. *The Georgia Gold Rush*. Columbia: University of South Carolina Press, 1993.

Wilson, James Grant, and John Fiske, eds. *Appletons' Cyclopaedia of American Biography*. New York: D. Appleton, 1889.

INDEX

Turner, William, 143, 144, 145, 147, 148, 150

ABOUT THE AUTHOR

During his four-and-a-half-decade writing career, James A. Crutchfield has published nearly seventy books pertaining to United States history and biography. His articles have appeared in magazines, newspapers, and journals across the country, earning multiple awards from *Library Journal,* the Daughters of the American Revolution, the American Association for State and Local History, and Western Writers of America. In 2011, Western Writers of America presented him with the Owen Wister Award for Lifetime Achievement in Western History and Literature. In 2015, Crutchfield was inducted into the Western Writers Hall of Fame, housed in the McCracken Research Library at the Buffalo Bill Center of the West in Cody, Wyoming. Crutchfield lives in Tennessee with his wife, Regena, and their three cats, Zoë, Oliver, and Rufus.